ENDGAME

ENDGAME

The Blueprint for Victory
in the War on Terror

Lt. General Thomas McInerney
USAF (Ret.)

Maj. General Paul Vallely
US Army (Ret.)

Since 1947
REGNERY
PUBLISHING, INC.
An Eagle Publishing Company • Washington, DC

Library of Congress Cataloging-in-Publication Data

McInerney, Thomas.
  Endgame : the blueprint for victory in the war on terror / Thomas McInerney and Paul E. Vallely.
      p. cm.
  ISBN 0-89526-066-2
  1. War on Terrorism, 2001– I. Vallely, Paul E. II. Title.
  HV6432.M387 2004
  973.931—dc22

                                                                    2004004909

Published in the United States by
Regnery Publishing, Inc.
An Eagle Publishing Company
One Massachusetts Avenue, NW
Washington, DC 20001
Visit us at www.regnery.com

Distributed to the trade by
National Book Network
4720-A Boston Way
Lanham, MD 20706

Printed on acid-free paper
Manufactured in the United States of America

10 9 8 7 6 5 4 3 2 1

Books are available in quantity for promotional or premium use. Write to Director of Special Sales, Regnery Publishing, Inc., One Massachusetts Avenue, NW, Washington, DC 20001, for information on discounts and terms or call (202) 216-0600.

CONTENTS

THE WEB OF TERROR

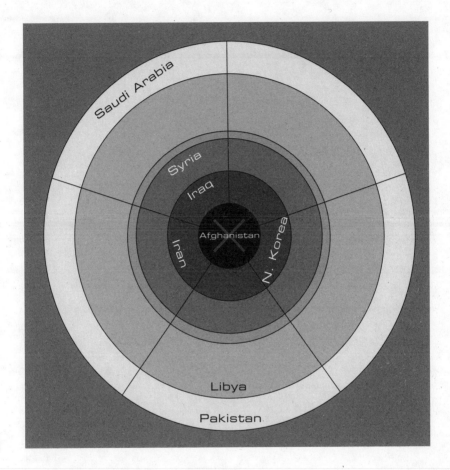

QUAGMIRE CHATTER

WHEN OPERATION IRAQI FREEDOM began, the chattering class of retired generals and admirals who appear regularly on U.S. television quickly fell into deep depression about a "quagmire" in Iraq. Retired generals trotted out as experts by the major media, among them Wesley Clark and Barry McCaffrey, prognosticated that the war would go on for months and that horrendous U.S. casualties should be expected. These armchair admirals, barroom brigadiers, and the sound-bite special forces theorized that General Tommy Franks had made "a monumental military blunder" by attacking Saddam with too small a force and inadequate "softening up" by air power before the ground offensive commenced. McCaffrey predicted that if there were a battle for Baghdad, the U.S. would probably take "a couple to three thousand casualties."

Clark and McCaffrey were wrong. In fact, the whole lot of the "babbling brass"—as the troops refer to these military mouthpieces for the mainstream media—were wrong. But there were two retired generals, commenting on the war for FOX News Channel, who knew better: Air Force Lieutenant General Tom McInerney and Major General Paul Vallely, U.S. Army. Tom McInerney last served as the assistant vice chief of staff of the Air Force and director of the defense performance review, and Paul Vallely last served as the Deputy Commanding General, U.S.

Army, Pacific. Both have extensive combat and command experience. A year before hostilities commenced in Iraq, these two well-informed officers astutely predicted a swift, favorable outcome in a "War of Liberation" for the Iraqi people. The McInerney-Vallely assessment was dead on—but ignored by "experts" like Wesley Clark and Barry McCaffrey and many other military pundits.

Clark, McCaffrey, and their cronies should have known better. When on active duty they had access to the same intelligence that McInerney and Vallely saw. They should have been just as aware as McInerney and Vallely were of developments on the international scene, as well as of advances in military technology. But instead of helping to show America how we could and would win the war on terror, they bought into and fed the prevailing defeatism of the mainstream media elites.

Chris Matthews warned that if the United States went to war with Iraq it "will join the Bay of Pigs, Vietnam, Desert One, Beirut, and Somalia in the history of military catastrophe." On March 29, 2003, just nine days into the war, the *New York Times* boldly proclaimed, "With every passing day, it is more evident that the allies made two gross military misjudgments in concluding that coalition forces could safely bypass Basra and An Nasiriyah and that Shi'ite Muslims in southern Iraq would rise up against Saddam Hussein." Unfortunately for the *Times*, the CENTCOM war plan didn't call for bypassing either city, nor did coalition forces expect or receive an "uprising" by any Iraqis.

Seymour Hersh, famous since Vietnam for his "investigative journalism," wrote in the March 31, 2003, edition of the *New Yorker*: "According to a dozen or so military men I spoke to, Rumsfeld simply failed to anticipate the consequences of protracted warfare. He put Army and Marine units in the field with few reserves and an insufficient number of tanks and other armored vehicles.... 'It's a stalemate now,' the former intelligence official told me."

One can only wonder who these "military men" were that Mr. Hersh spoke to. In the aftermath of Baghdad's collapse just nine days

later, most of the media turned on a dime and began criticizing Secretary Rumsfeld for not anticipating the consequences of a short-dura-
tion war.

The defeatism and anti-American rhetoric reached its height in the
activity of journalist Peter Arnett. I was in Iraq on March 31, 2003,
when word spread among the troops about comments Arnett had
made during an interview he had given on Iraqi state television.
Arnett was well known for his coverage of the first Gulf War for CNN
and for a televised "documentary" piece called "Tailwind," which
falsely alleged that U.S. forces had illegally used nerve gas in Vietnam.
Fairly or not, Arnett is widely perceived by many in the ranks to be
antimilitary. Now he was in Baghdad "reporting" for NBC and
National Geographic, and apparently apologizing to the Iraqis for the
U.S.-led invasion.

Though few of the troops actually saw the broadcast of Arnett being
interviewed by an Iraqi in military uniform, almost everyone had
heard some of what he had said. "The first U.S. war plan has failed
because of Iraqi resistance. Now they are trying to write another war
plan. Clearly, the American war planners misjudged the determination of the Iraqi forces."

From what we were picking up on our satellite transceiver, the
interview precipitated an uproar back in the United States. In Iraq, the
troops wondered out loud why, with all our precision-guided munitions, Iraqi state television was still on the air. As for Arnett, they
regarded his comments to be treasonous, a personal affront, and took
to describing his lineage in unprintable terms.

But Arnett was not a singular case. In fact, most of the overseas
media in Iraq, who parroted what "talking head" generals like Clark
and McCafferey were "reporting" from Atlanta, New York, and Washington, were just as defeatist as Arnett was. And most of the international press seemed interested only in describing our young warriors
in Iraq in negative terms. Even the likes of former national security
advisor General Brent Scowcroft did not "get it." McInerney and

Vallely "got it" right from the beginning. The pundits swirled around the young troopers like sharks looking for prey. Questions flew about everything from the weather to opinions on the UN, antiwar protests, their commander in chief, and how long they had had to sit around in Iraq waiting for the war to start.

Before the war began on March 20, these masters of the media and their outlets in the United States spread unfounded reports that our troops in Iraq were unprepared and ill equipped for the mission that lay ahead. The bevy of "experts," including the network "brass hats," added fuel to this fire by saying that our chemical protective suits didn't work and that there weren't enough troops, the right weapons, or enough equipment to take on Saddam's 480,000-man military. Some went so far as to suggest that the "mission focus" of these young Americans in uniform stemmed from their being "brainwashed" by their superiors.

A number of foreign journalists described the Marines I was with as "bloodthirsty." I heard one female correspondent asking—or was it telling?—one of the Marine minders that she had "never seen so much bravado, machismo, or arrogance" in her life. The young NCO listened to her complaint, appeared to mull over her grievance, and then replied, "Yes, ma'am, that's why they call themselves United States Marines."

POSTWAR QUAGMIRE

The same defeatism and negativity dominated the airwaves and newsprint after the fall of Baghdad, giving Americans and the world a false picture of post-Saddam Iraq. Said Dan Rather: "While increasingly organized guerilla-style attacks are a top concern for American forces in Iraq, ordinary Iraqis are faced with an extraordinary surge of crime, banditry, and thuggery, from carjacking and robbery to kidnapping and murder. The result is a population fearful, frustrated, angry, and heavily armed."

Dan's colleague Kimberly Dozier followed this with a few whoppers of her own: "Day or night, these are some of the most dangerous streets on Earth. Desperation drives murder and theft. Iraqis have traded fear of the despot for fear of their fellow man, and U.S. troops seem powerless to protect them."

Newsweek irresponsibly compared Defense Secretary Donald Rumsfeld to "Baghdad Bob." *New York Times* reporter Richard Bernstein said President Bush was seen as "a gun-slinging cowboy knocking over international treaties and bent on controlling the world's oil, if not the entire world."

As summer turned to fall in 2003, *Time* magazine ran four cover stories in three months attacking the president's efforts in Iraq. July 14: "Peace Is Hell." July 21: "Untruth and Consequences." September 1: "Are We Stretched Too Thin?" Worst of all was their October 6 issue. It featured a photo of President Bush after landing aboard the carrier USS *Lincoln*. The caption? "Mission NOT Accomplished." The title of the story inside the magazine: "So, What Went Wrong?"

Such negative reports, warned Rep. Jim Marshall (D-GA), when he returned from a fact-finding trip to Baghdad, were "hurting our chances" to complete the mission in Iraq. "The falsely bleak picture" painted by the media, Marshall wrote, "weakens our national resolve, discourages Iraqi cooperation and emboldens our enemy."

Not only that. They even confused our own personnel. When the "experts" were filling the airwaves with dire predictions that the war in Iraq could cost up to three thousand American and British deaths, I saw the impact it had on our young men and women in Iraq. The word "quagmire" was thrown around as if coalition forces were bogged down in a swamp. Commentators loved comparing the situation to Vietnam.

One night I was watching the news on our tiny satellite transceiver, surrounded by some of our troops. At one point a trooper looked up and asked me, "Is that right, Colonel North? You were in Vietnam. Is this what happened there?"

He was clearly too young to have been alive while I was at Khe Sanh or Con Thein, or to know much about Hue city, or the fifty-nine-day-long Tet offensive of 1968 when we took sixty-four U.S. casualties a day. So I tried to explain how different the two wars really were.

"From their safe haven in North Vietnam, the rulers in Hanoi, supported by Communist China and the Soviet Union, invaded South Vietnam with conventional military forces and simultaneously orchestrated an indigenous insurgency," I told him. "Other than a bombing campaign, we never seriously threatened Hanoi. That's not the case here in Iraq, where we're taking the fight directly to the despot who has attacked his neighbors and oppressed the Iraqi people for more than three decades. Here we face a conventional indigenous army and some 'guerillas'—mostly foreign fedayeen on a jihad.

"In Vietnam, the Viet Cong guerillas were operating as a 'wholly owned subsidiary' of the North Vietnamese. Here, we're being attacked by criminals released from prison just before the war started and by Ba'athists who want to restore their power and prestige by orchestrating the attacks, along with jihadist foreign fedayeen who are coming here to become 'martyrs.' But none of these groups are coordinating their efforts and activities."

The young Marine nodded, seeming to understand the differences. That's more than could be said for most of the news directors, editors, and publishers back in the States. This disconnect from reality also appeared in coverage of the David Kay report. Kay, a top U.S. weapons inspector, released a preliminary report early in 2004, stating that his team had uncovered widespread evidence of unreported biological and chemical weapons programs that were concealed from UN inspectors. In Kay's words, "Iraq's WMD [weapons of mass destruction] programs spanned more than two decades, involved thousands of people, billions of dollars, and were elaborately shielded by security and deception operations that continued even beyond the end of Operation Iraqi Freedom."

His report stated that "over two dozen laboratories that were hidden by the Iraqi intelligence service...had prohibited equipment, and ... at the minimum, kept alive Iraq's capability to produce both biological and chemical weapons."

But Kay also noted that much of the evidence of WMD "is irretrievably lost" because prior to the war there was "deliberate dispersal and destruction of material and documentation related to weapons programs." In spite of these clear statements, the *Washington Post* ran this headline: "Search in Iraq Finds No Banned Weapons."

Negative news reports are creating the impression that U.S. and coalition forces are losing in Iraq. Those who have been there, like Tom McInerney and Paul Vallely, know that is not the case.

After I returned from Iraq, John Wobensmith, retired from the National Security Agency and now with the Institute of World Politics, made a five-city tour of Iraq. His assessment confirmed what I had seen and reported: that the attitude of the Iraqi people toward Americans and our allies is "very positive." He said the reports of chaos are "greatly exaggerated" and "tremendous progress" is being made.

The media have also created the impression that the United States is going it alone in Iraq. Yet more than three dozen countries are contributing to the military and reconstruction effort. More than twenty countries have sent personnel. Even Japan, a country not yet directly attacked by jihadist terrorsm, has deployed peacekeepers.

The media has also created the impression that Saddam had no military arsenal. Yet as I reported from Bayji—a refinery city northwest of Tikrit—the ammunition depot captured by the 3rd Battalion, 66th Armor has more than 300 million tons of ammunition in it. And the Bayji ASP (Ammunition Storage Point) is but one of more than one hundred similar installations.

The media has also created the impression that there is still an impenetrable, sophisticated Iraqi resistance. Yet as of mid-February 2004, all but ten of the top fifty-five most wanted Ba'athists have been captured or killed.

If you watch the news even today, you might conclude that there is little to no infrastructure. But in fact, more Iraqis have electricity, running water, and sewage service today than at any time in the history of the country. All twenty-two universities and forty-three technical institutes are open. Nearly all primary and secondary schools are open. All 240 hospitals and more than 1200 clinics are in operation. Coalition medical personnel have helped administer more than twenty-two million vaccinations to Iraqi children, and new malaria cases have dropped to a historic low.

All this and much more has been accomplished in free Iraq in less than ten months after Saddam was driven from Baghdad. Not a bad record for a region where dictatorships are measured in decades. And not a bad story if the news media had cared to report it.

SADDAM QUAGMIRE

The most egregious example of all of the media's defeatism in the war on terror occurred when Saddam Hussein was captured. American soldiers trapped him like a cornered rat hiding in a hole. And when he was caught, this blustering, bloody tyrant who asked others to die for him didn't even try to defend himself with the weapons at his disposal.

Just days before the capture, I interviewed Major Gen. Ray Odierno, commanding general of the 4th Infantry Division, for FOX News Channel, who told me that his troops would find Saddam near Tikrit. They did. But what the general didn't predict was that the apprehension of this mass murderer would apparently drive many liberal Democrats and their friends in the media around the bend.

The day after Saddam was videotaped being examined for lice by a U.S. Army doctor, Howard Dean, at that time the front-runner among then nine Democratic presidential candidates, declared, "The capture of Saddam Hussein is good news for the Iraqi people and the world. Saddam was a brutal dictator who should be brought swiftly to justice for his crimes." All true. But then Dean, who once mused aloud about whether President Bush knew about the September 11 attack before it happened, went on to say that he remained opposed to what we're doing in Iraq because "the administration launched the war in the wrong way, at the wrong time, with inadequate planning, insufficient help, and at an unbelievable cost."

It's no wonder Dean's campaign sank so fast. He followed the intellectual inconsistency of this statement with an even more schizophrenic assertion. On the one hand he said, "The capture of Saddam is a good thing, which I hope very much will help keep our soldiers safer." But! "But the capture of Saddam has not made America safer." He has never explained why America was no safer with the Butcher of Baghdad behind bars.

Unfortunately, Howard Dean wasn't the only liberal Democrat with a peculiar perception of Iraqi reality. Two days after Paul Bremer proclaimed, "We got him," Rep. Jim McDermott (D-WA) accused President Bush of manipulating the capture of Saddam for political purposes. McDermott told a Seattle radio audience that U.S. troops could have captured Saddam "a long time ago if they wanted." He went on to posit, "It's funny, when they're having all this trouble, suddenly they have to roll out something."

Bizarre? No more so than Clinton-era Secretary of State Madeleine Albright's assertion to Morton Kondracke of FOX News Channel a few days later: "Do you suppose that the Bush administration has Osama bin Laden hidden away somewhere and will bring him out before the election?" Asked if she was joking, Kondracke replied, "She was not smiling."

Media coverage of the capture was as surreal as the Democrats' conspiracy conjectures. After watching jubilant Iraqis celebrating Saddam's apprehension, ABC anchor Peter Jennings saw only sadness. He morosely concluded, "There's not a good deal for Iraqis to be happy about at the moment." Jennings "informed" the American public that life for Iraqi citizens is "very chaotic...beset by violence...[and] not as stable for them as it was when Saddam Hussein was in power."

The anchors and talking heads pondered Saddam's trial and concluded that it could be "embarrassing" to the United States.

CBS's Leslie Stahl nagged Defense Secretary Donald Rumsfeld with questions about whether we would torture Saddam. "Would we deprive him of sleep? Would we make it very cold where he is, or very hot? Are there any restrictions on the way we treat him to get him to cooperate more than he has been?"

NBC's Katie Couric said Saddam's capture was only "symbolic." She would be proved hopelessly wrong less than twenty-four hours later, when the 1st Armored Division—acting on intelligence secured from Saddam's capture—rounded up three former Iraqi generals who had been supporting the terrorist resistance in Iraq.

All of this twisted, blame-America Bush-bashing and mind-numbing negativism has obscured some very important facts that need to be reemphasized:

Saddam is responsible for two horrific wars and the deaths of hundreds of thousands. His record is replete with the kind of atrocities that brought the United States into two world wars, a bloody campaign in Korea, and the war I fought in: Vietnam. He raped, tortured, robbed, starved, and murdered his own people. The filthiest slum I ever saw was Baghdad's Saddam City. The Iraqi dictator mandated that the Shi'ites who fled to the capital of Iraq had to live in the "planned community" he named after himself. It was a rabbit warren of crumbling, multistory, Soviet-style apartment buildings without running water or functioning sewage systems. It was worse than anything I've ever seen in Calcutta, Haiti, or Bangladesh. Yet the place was home to more than a million "internal refugees," teeming with naked children, their stomachs distended from malnutrition. There was raw sewage running in the streets, and piles of trash—some of it smoldering with a stench that was enough to make even Marines who hadn't bathed in weeks smell good.

Saddam acquired and used WMDs against his neighbors and countrymen. In the Kurdish areas of northern Iraq, there are eyewitnesses to what Saddam's chemical weapons can do. In 1988, he unleashed poison gas in Kurdish areas—and that was only the beginning. By the time he was finished he was responsible for killing 250,000 Kurds and just as many Shi'ites in the south. His brutality also created more than two million refugees. Scores of villages in the north and south of the country were emptied of every living soul. Unlike most of their former colleagues in the media, McInerney and Vallely don't have an agenda. They understand these things. They've been there. And as the troops say, they "get it."

TAKING ON TERROR

When nineteen Islamic terrorists seized four U.S. airliners and killed at least 2,731 people on American soil that terrible Tuesday, I was on Northwest Airlines flight 238 headed into Reagan National. While we were en route to Washington's closest airport, American Airlines Flight 77, which had been hijacked as it departed Dulles Airport a few minutes earlier, slammed into the west wall of the Pentagon at 0937. My flight was immediately diverted to Dulles, and I eventually arrived at the FOX News Channel studios in Washington hours later. By the time we finally finished broadcasting that night around midnight, questions were already being raised about what role Saddam might have played in the attack.

A month later, I was aboard the USS *Bataan* with the Marines who were preparing to make a heloborne assault into Kandahar, Afghanistan, to take on the Taliban and Osama bin Laden's al-Qaeda, and those questions were still being asked. A short while after I returned home, other U.S. forces found evidence that bin Laden had been trying to acquire nuclear material. Could he have gotten some from Iraq?

Over two years after the Twin Towers in New York were brought down into two terrible piles of rubble and bodies, the answer still is not known.

What is known is that Saddam Hussein openly defied the United Nations weapons inspectors. The hapless Hans Blix finally gave up even the pretense of being able to conduct a realistic investigation into what Saddam may or may not have done with his tons of poison gas, chemical warheads, anthrax, and nuclear materials. Without credible human sources inside Iraq, no U.S. or British intelligence agency knows for certain either. But in the aftermath of September 11, the fear of Saddam using any of these—or giving them to others to use in a terrorist attack—was palpable in the governments of the United States and Great Britain.

Can't find the WMDs? If asked, the troops who have been searching for WMDs will remind the questioner that Saddam had more than five months to destroy, remove, or hide anything he wanted before U.S. and British troops arrived on his doorstep. They will also point to the terror-bomb jackets, terrorist training manuals, and large numbers of foreign terrorists who were trained at Salman Pak. They will present the tons of chemical protective equipment, atropine injectors, decontamination equipment, and chemical warfare manuals that they found all over Iraq and ask, "If Saddam didn't have chemical agents, how come his troops had all this gear?"

Saddam also attempted to assassinate an American president. He trained and supported Hamas, Islamic Jihad, Hezbollah, and Muslim Brotherhood terrorists who killed Americans. Are we to believe that al-Qaeda was the only Islamic terror group that Saddam did not support?

The image of Saddam as a filthy, decrepit, coward captured—not killed—by an American soldier is a powerful message to repressed people all over the globe that this is the way brutal despots go. Placing him on trial before the people of Iraq—not in The Hague or somewhere else—sends a clear signal to totalitarians and terrorists (be they in Damascus, Tehran, Pyongyang, Havana, or hiding in the hills) that they are accountable to the people they have tortured and terrified.

Now, the most committed followers of Osama bin Laden have cause to wonder if their bearded leader who wants them to die for his cause would ignominiously surrender himself to the tender mercies of the International Criminal Court to avoid an untimely demise.

Finally, the loopy leftist rhetoric in the aftermath of Saddam's capture obscures the extraordinary courage, training, persistence, and discipline of the American soldiers who pursued and caught the Butcher
of Baghdad. In reality, none of the soldiers, sailors, airmen, or Marines
with whom I spoke in Iraq were even close to the bloodthirsty, trigger-
happy thugs that all too many media types try to suggest (or state out-
right) that they are. None of them ever told me they were "itching for
a fight." What was missed by most of the media in Iraq was the fact
that no one who has ever really been to a war ever really wants to go
to another one. And as McInerney and Vallely point out, a remarkable
percentage of the young men there already had combat experience.
One commander I spoke with estimated that nearly half his officers
and senior non-commissioned officers had served under fire before—
in the first Gulf War, the Balkans, or Afghanistan, and in some cases,
all three. They knew better than any correspondent, reporter, or politi-
cian the true nature of war: that it is the most terrible of human
endeavors.

Yet precisely because so many of them had combat experience, they
were anxious to get on with the task at hand, and do so efficiently.
They became the first to demonstrate the new approaches that the military is developing to meet the terror threat.

And Tom McInerney and Paul Vallely actually listened to them.

One principal reason why McInerney and Vallely were and are different from the defeatist media claque is that they took the trouble to
talk with the people on "the sharp edge," as they put it: "in the rifle
companies, artillery batteries, tank platoons, quartermaster battalions,
Special Forces A-teams, bomber wings, airlift squadrons, communications detachments, fighter squadrons, aircraft carriers, submarines,
cruisers, destroyers, and amphibious warfare ships."

I know they're right because I've listened to them, too. Like Tom
McInerney and Paul Vallely, I know the men and women who have
done the fighting for us in Iraq. As they battled into Iraq and toppled
Saddam's regime, I was with them, eating the same meals, breathing

the same dust, sharing their fears, frustrations, and euphoria—and enjoying their protection.

The conditions under which they achieved our great victory in Iraq—which surprised the world as much as it must have surprised Wes Clark, Barry McCaffrey, and Katie Couric—were difficult in the extreme. One day I found Marine maintenance technicians wearing gas masks so that they could work on aircraft during the worst dust storm I've ever experienced. The wind, blowing steadily at twenty-five to thirty knots, was howling like a banshee through antenna guy wires. The storm had the strange effect of turning daylight into dusk, blotting out the sun, and giving an orange hue to every structure, man, and machine. Visibility was less than twenty yards. The air appeared foggy, the way it does along the Atlantic or Pacific Coast when there is a large storm offshore. But the "fog" in the air wasn't water vapor, it was dirt—tiny particles of sand that the Marines inhaled with every breath and swallowed with every mouthful of food. During sand-storms in Iraq it whips through the air, jamming weapons, seeping into every crevice, and clogging the intakes of jet engines and the fil-ters of the gas masks we all carried everywhere, all the time. But when asked if the dust and dirt would affect the performance of his aircraft, the Marine maintenance tech calmly replied, "Dust storms aren't allowed to affect us. It's contrary to Marine Corps policy."

He was joking, but there was a serious edge to his reply: He knew that America was in the Iraqi fight for keeps, whatever the obstacles. We would not be beaten. It was contrary to policy.

DEMOCRAT QUAGMIRE

That policy transcends politics, and should have bipartisan support. The strategies McInerney and Vallely outline here are vital for nothing less than the continued survival of the United States and its people. They're all the more impo. tant as partisanship intrudes increasingly into national security issues. Recently, a Democratic Party plan to unseat the president of the United States was discovered. It was found in the offices of the Senate Select Committee on Intelligence, and had apparently been written by a Democrat staffer on the committee.

The document outlined a political plan to use the Senate Intelligence Committee to ramp up opposition to the war on terror, President Bush, and his administration. The apparent goal: to unseat the president by using the committee as a tool to divide the commander in chief from the troops he leads. "We have carefully reviewed our options," and "the best approach," the memo states, is to urge investigations of the "Office of the Secretary of Defense as well as Secretary Bolton's office at the State Department."

Back in June 2003, the committee decided to evaluate documented intelligence regarding Iraq's WMD programs. Its review was supposed to examine shortcomings in the U.S. intelligence community—something both Democrats and Republicans agree are plentiful—and to formulate, in a responsible and bipartisan way, recommendations for improvement. Assuming that this effort might lead to much-needed enhancements in our ability to collect human intelligence amid a war that has already claimed more than 3,000 American lives, such a review makes sense. Nearly all responsible politicians agree that our intelligence community desperately needs better ways of penetrating radical Islamist terror cells. Even those running for office acknowledge that we are in a war in which young Americans are dying—a war in which the lack of good intelligence is our greatest liability.

Therefore, it seems that the primary responsibility of the Senate Select Committee on Intelligence should be to discern what needs fixing within our intelligence community and determine with urgency what resources are needed for those improvements. After all, the lives of young Americans in Afghanistan and Iraq—as well as the safety of U.S. citizens at home—hang in the balance.

But this memorandum reveals that these goals are not even being considered by eight of the seventeen members of the Senate's Intelligence Committee. The Democrats who sit on one of the most sensitive and important bodies in our government have apparently decided that gathering, assessing, and analyzing intelligence is less important than booting this president from office. "Intelligence issues are clearly secondary to the public's concern regarding the insurgency in Iraq," the memo states. In short, they have abandoned their responsibilities to our soldiers, sailors, airmen, Marines, and countrymen and decided instead to wage war against the president.

Those who really care about winning the real war in which we are now engaged should be outraged at this crass politicization of a committee so closely tied to our national security. Thank God, some Democrats are. Senator Joe Lieberman, even before he dropped out of the contest for his party's presidential nomination, decried the memorandum as "unsavory." Senator Zell Miller went even further. "If this is not treason," the Georgia Democrat said, "it's the first cousin of treason."

But Al Gore called it "trivial."

The memo suggests that Democrats "pull the trigger" on their plan at the height of the 2004 presidential election campaign. But the Bush haters couldn't wait—they're already in full attack mode. Rep. Charlie Rangel (D-NY) introduced a formal resolution asking the president to give the Bronx cheer to Don Rumsfeld and send him packing. Immediately, twenty-five of Charlie's pals in the House notified him that they, too, wanted a piece of Rumsfeld's scalp as a treasure to parade before their rabid supporters. Rangel and his merry band of headhunters accuse Rumsfeld of "gross mismanagement," "repeated miscalculations," a "lack of sensitivity," and having "misled the American people"—everything but stealing food from Iraqi children.

Among those accusing Rumsfeld of gross negligence are such luminaries as Reps. Pete Stark (D-CA), who once tried to goad Republicans on the Ways and Means Committee into a fistfight; Jim McDermott (D-WA), who provided propaganda for Saddam's government with a visit to Iraq in October 2002; Dennis Kucinich (D-OH), who believes his proposed "Department of Peace" is the panacea for the world's many dangers; and Barbara Lee (D-CA), the only member of the House who voted against responding to the murder of 3,000 of our fellow Americans by going to war in Afghanistan.

Thankfully, these members of Congress do not constitute our first line of defense against terrorism. But clearly the Bush haters were emboldened by the presidential attack plan. "They have decided to put partisanship ahead of our nation's security," said Intelligence Committee Chairman Pat Roberts (R-KS).

Unfortunately, the partisanship doesn't stop with efforts to twist the outcome of a presidential election. Some of it is aimed at the troops fighting the war. "Congress is not an ATM," snapped West Virginia Senator Robert Byrd in response to the president's request for $87 billion to fight the war on terrorism. Byrd, the ranking member on the Senate Appropriations Committee and the King of Pork, has never met a tax dollar he didn't want to spend—especially if it was for a road or building bearing his name in West Virginia. Yet Byrd, who has used public money to put his name on more arches than Ronald McDonald, says that when it comes to protecting our national security, he refuses to "simply rubber-stamp" the president's request.

One might have hoped that partisan selfishness would have been unheard of while we're at war, but Byrd was not alone. Senator John Breaux, a "moderate" Democrat, was even blunter about his desire to spend money not on defense but on what will help him get reelected. With patriotic fervor and far-sightedness, he declared, "I got things that need to be built in Louisiana." Rep. Rahm Emanuel demanded that for every dollar spent on efforts in Iraq and Afghanistan, an equal amount be spent on domestic projects. Teddy Kennedy agreed, suggesting that instead of spending money to root out terrorists who want to kill Americans, the money should be used to train teachers who can't teach and for a universal health care system that's already been rejected by the American people.

When asked in summer 2003 to comment on the killing of a Marine in Iraq, President Bush replied, "There are some who feel that the conditions are such that they can attack us there...Bring 'em on!...Our forces are ready." This prompted New Jersey Democratic Senator Frank Lautenberg to jump for the nearest microphone and proclaim that he was shaking his head "in disbelief." He then sputtered that when he was in World War II he had "never heard any military commander—let alone the commander in chief—invite enemies to attack U.S. troops."

Mr. Lautenberg must think that at Bastogne, General Anthony McAuliffe was asking the Germans for hors d'oeuvres when he replied to their surrender demand with "Nuts."

After hearing Senator Lautenberg and the explanations of the pollsters, I decided to conduct my own informal, admittedly unscientific sampling of American public opinion to see how deeply this sense of national dyspepsia was being felt. I called a military recruiter. "The polls say Americans are growing disheartened," I told him. "Are you seeing any dropoff in volunteers?"

"Not here. We have all the high-school graduates we need for the next two months," he replied, knowing that he was one of those responsible for enlisting 185,000 new recruits in 2003.

The conversation reminded me of one I had on-air with a young lance corporal just east of Baghdad in early April 2003. The *New York Times* had reported that morning that the Marines had outrun their supply lines and were out of food, water, fuel, and ammo. I stood next to the youthful Leatherneck, told him about the story, stuck the microphone in his face, and asked, "Are you hungry?"

"No, sir."

"Thirsty?"

"No, sir."

"Are you short on ammo?"

"No, sir."

"Well, what do you need?" I pressed.

"Just send more enemy, sir."

Bravado? Sure. But it's real, right from the lips of one of those who stand in harm's way defending us—and offering the hope of freedom to others.

It was that same kind of audacity that inspired fifty-six patriots to gather in a hot hall in Philadelphia that July of 1776 and stick it in King George's eye. They knew it was going to be a rough go, but they didn't shirk and whine. They signed on to the notion that we are endowed by our Creator "with certain unalienable Rights, that among these are Life, Liberty and the Pursuit of Happiness." But unlike much of the modern media—and too many of today's liberal politicians—they were willing to fight for it.

THE IRAQ-TERROR CONNECTION—
THE WEB OF TERROR

Democrats might do well to remember that enjoying "the blessings of Liberty" sometimes requires us to cinch up our belts, suck it up, and get on with the business of protecting ourselves. Yet it seems even today that too many Democrats simply don't understand that the United States is engaged in a war against jihadist terrorists: enemies of civilization like al-Qaeda, Hamas, Islamic Jihad, and others. They think that if we just capture Osama bin Laden, the world will return to normal.

Once again, they should check in with McInerney and Vallely. In *Endgame*, they explain how these terrorists operate. Radical Muslim group members don't all report to one man. The groups act much like franchise operations. They are recruited locally, trained at "Terrorism University" for a few months, and sent out into the world to go into business for themselves. In Iraq, we saw how tenacious they were. When Saddam's Republican Guard regulars cut and ran before advancing American and coalition troops, the foreign jihadis stood their ground and fought tenaciously—often to the death. In Iraq I saw Syrian, Jordanian, Saudi, Egyptian, Lebanese, and Yemeni fighters who were absolutely unafraid to die—in fact, they wanted to die—and unshakably committed to the cause of jihad. I saw many Iraqi prisoners taken elsewhere, but on one occasion when a band of jihadis engaged our troops along a stretch of Iraqi highway, I saw only two of them taken alive. Both were badly wounded.

The war in Iraq is a great victory in the war against these jihadis— a struggle that has been going on, at varying degrees of intensity, for decades. In fact, Iraq has proven to be "the wrong place at the wrong time" for all manner of Middle Eastern terror organizations. Before the war started, Abu Nidal, the vicious assassin who had tried to kill me, my wife, and children, was found dead in Baghdad. The Al Aksr Martyrs Brigade, the suicide terror wing of Hamas, lost much of its financial support when Saddam folded his tent.

And in one case, while I was in Iraq covering the Marine advance on Baghdad, it was very personal. One morning I was sitting on the ramp of an AAV washing my feet and changing my socks—one of those pleasant, solitary rituals that infantry Marines try to practice daily but often don't get to—when I got the message from Griff Jenkins, my combat cameraman and field producer: "CENTCOM says the Marines down south have captured 'Abu somebody' you were looking for."

"Abu who?" I asked, somewhat irritated that my ablutions were being interrupted.

"I don't know," he replied. "Here," he said, handing me a phone, "talk to New York."

The name was Abu Abbas. He had been captured by Marine and Task Force 20 operators during a raid on the outskirts of Baghdad. Abbas was the Palestinian terrorist who masterminded the October 1985 hijacking of the Italian *Achille Lauro* cruise ship. When I served as the U.S. government's coordinator for counterterrorism, I was deeply involved in efforts to capture Abbas and his three fellow terrorists.

It was an operation in which those who claimed to be our friends thwarted the United States at every turn. (Sounds like today, doesn't it?) Egyptian president Hosni Mubarak was the first. He lied to Ronald Reagan, and then tried to facilitate the terrorists' escape.

Abbas, the head of the Palestine Liberation Front, had orchestrated the hijacking of the ship and the cold-blooded murder of Leon Klinghoffer. A sixty-nine-year-old invalid, Klinghoffer was shot while he sat in his wheelchair; his body was then dumped overboard. The Egyptians allowed the ship to sail into Alexandria harbor, where officials dispatched by Mubarak took the terrorists off the ship and hid them while arranging for an EgyptAir DC-9 to secretly fly them out of the country.

President Reagan called Mubarak and told him, "I understand the terrorists are in Egypt. I want them."

Mubarak denied they were still there and claimed that he was sorry and that he didn't know that they killed anyone. Meanwhile, the terrorists were secretly moved to the airport for a flight to Tunis, Tunisia, where Yasser Arafat was quietly preparing a hero's welcome.

With help from the Israeli intelligence services, we confirmed information we had received about the EgyptAir escape aircraft with the terrorists aboard. The plane was then intercepted over the Mediterranean Sea by F-14s from the 6th Fleet and escorted to the NATO base at Sigonella, Sicily.

When the EgyptAir commercial airliner touched down at Sigonella, it was immediately surrounded by a Special Operations unit led by Brig. Gen. Carl Steiner, who boldly opened the aircraft door, faced down the armed guard and terrorists, and took them into custody. As the SEALs prepared to escort the four terrorists to a waiting USAF C-141, they were themselves surrounded by Italian police. To avoid a "friendly fire" incident with our Italian "allies," Steiner was ordered to turn the Palestinian terrorists over to the police.

Once again, President Reagan was on the phone—this time with Italy's Prime Minister Bettino Craxi, who promised that all four would be tried for hijacking and murder. Craxi lied.

The three "trigger men" were detained, but Abbas, dressed in the uniform of an airline pilot, was secretly put aboard a Yugoslav airliner and flown to Yugoslavia. From there the PLF terror chieftain flew to Tunisia to meet his old buddy Arafat. A few months later, fearing that the Israelis might be closing in on Abbas, Arafat arranged for him to move to Damascus and from there to Baghdad.

President George W. Bush had named Abbas in a speech last fall as part of his argument for removing Saddam Hussein from power. "Iraq has . . . provided safe haven to Abu Abbas," he said, then added, "And we know that Iraq is continuing to finance terror and gives assistance to groups that use terrorism to undermine Middle East peace."

The PLF faction led by Abbas had been a conduit for the money Saddam provided to the families of Palestinian suicide bombers—it's believed that millions of dollars have been provided for this purpose.

After nearly two decades, I can still hear President Ronald Reagan's words when he told the nation what had happened on the *Achille Lauro*: "You can run, but you can't hide."

Capturing Abbas was one victory, but there are many others like him still out there. As Tom McInerney and Paul Vallely accurately point out, this is the foe we are up against in the war on terror: a determined, unyielding, unrelenting enemy that is extremely adept at hiding—all around the world—within the larger community of Islamic jihadist sympathizers. The jihadis we fought in Baghdad yesterday could turn up in Paris today—or Washington tomorrow.

On my second trip to Iraq I went to Saddam's palace in Tikrit to interview Army Colonel Joe Campbell, commander of the 4th Infantry Division's 3rd Brigade, about how he saw things shaping up.

"Our biggest challenge right now is civil affairs," Campbell told me. "We've got to get the infrastructure up and running again. We're working civil affairs to win the hearts and minds of the Iraqi civilians," he said, and then added, "American soldiers are here to liberate. And it doesn't matter how long it takes." (At least as long as the Democrats don't get back into the White House.)

When I asked Colonel Campbell what the most difficult aspect of the war was for him, he said, "I think it's tougher now because you don't know who the enemy is. He's dressed like the normal civilian in the city, so you really have to keep your guard up. And you have to be vigilant in terms of how you execute your missions and have to keep your eyes and ears open."

Good advice—and not just for Iraq. This is the kind of warfare for which McInerney and Vallely formulate a strategy in this book. It is much needed, and indeed, long overdue. For while Senate staff members, angry Democratic congressmen, and liberal billionaires continue their partisan tirades today, brave Americans are still in harm's way in a war against terrorists that we must win. Former CIA director James Woolsey maintains that "the war on terrorism is World War IV—a war we cannot afford to lose." Recently retired General Tommy Franks, who commanded CENTCOM through Operation Enduring Freedom in Afghanistan and then led Operation Iraqi Freedom through to the liberation of Iraq, told me on October 10, 2003, that "the war on terrorism is going to go on for a long, long time."

He went on to point out that victory in Iraq is an important step in that war. He's right. Those we face aren't just willing to die for their cause—they want to die for their cause. They have been taught to hate, to kill, and to die in trying to kill Americans, Christians, and Jews. They have been promised spiritual rewards for themselves and financial benefits for their families if they succeed in killing themselves the "right way." Transforming Iraq into a secure democracy with a thriving economy will mean one less place where terrorists can be recruited or trained or take refuge.

But we will fail if these shortsighted political games continue.

UN QUAGMIRE

Calls to bring home the troops, cut off funds, and hand things over to the UN are selfish and short-sighted. Democrats continue to salivate at the prospect that the UN may yet get to run Iraq. The only way to defend America's national security, they have argued, is to "internationalize" the rebuilding of Iraq and place our fate in the hands of Kofi Annan. It is now liberal dogma to trust the UN more than the United States government.

As charter members of the UN Fan Club, liberals contend that UN peacekeepers can stabilize Iraq better than the U.S. military. They believe Kofi Annan is more committed and better equipped to defeat terrorism than George W. Bush; and want the UN Security Council, not the U.S. Congress, to be the final arbiter on sending American troops into war.

In fact, the Bush administration has asked the UN for help in the war on terrorism and in rebuilding Iraq. But like a spoiled child on the playground, the UN wants no part of those efforts if it can't be in charge and amass power.

That hasn't stopped those who want to wrest the mantle of "commander in chief" from George Bush from insisting that we "bring the boys home" and put the UN in charge of protecting America from terrorism. Presidential candidate John Kerry seems perfectly happy to subordinate U.S. interests to the UN. In his campaign speeches, Kerry sounds more like a candidate for UN secretary-general than for president of the United States. Standing in South Carolina's "Patriot's Point," he explained that denying the UN a leadership role in rebuilding a country that American soldiers, sailors, airmen, and Marines liberated was a "miscalculation of colossal proportions." He routinely demands that the Bush administration "return to the United Nations with genuine respect" and explains that when he voted to authorize war in Iraq, it was to "make Saddam Hussein comply with the resolutions of the United Nations." He doesn't mention if U.S. security interests factored into his decision.

Senate Minority Leader Tom Daschle apparently agrees with Kerry. He has said that bringing the UN into the Iraq equation has "been a long time in coming."

But the Democrats have it backwards. The UN sought at every turn to obstruct and delegitimize any decisive action against Saddam Hussein's regime. Starting in the summer of 2002, our "allies"—the French, the Germans, and most of "Old Europe"—began employing every tactic possible in the UN to prevent the use of force in Iraq. Encouraged by massive anti-American protests on the streets of European capitals, President Jacques Chirac of France and Chancellor Gerhard Schroeder of Germany repeatedly demanded that the United States and Great Britain delay any plans for military action against Saddam Hussein until UN supersleuth Hans Blix had "completed" his search for weapons of mass destruction in Iraq.

By the autumn of 2002, U.S. frustration with the snail's pace of Blix's mission was dismissed as "saber rattling" in Paris, Berlin, and Brussels and on the UN cocktail party circuit. And at the UN, it's all about power. Before the war, Secretary-General Kofi Annan insisted that any military effort to oust Saddam without UN permission would lack "the unique legitimacy provided by the United Nations." After Baghdad fell, Annan demanded that the UN be allowed to exercise control over how U.S. forces and U.S. tax dollars were employed and spent in Iraq.

All this belies the abysmal, decade-long record of the UN in the land between the rivers. The UN-administered Oil-for-Food Program, established in 1995 to provide the Iraqi people with food and medicine, was totally corrupt. Under UN supervision, Saddam stole billions from the program while UN administrators took tens of millions in "management fees." We now know that hundreds of millions of dollars skimmed from the Oil-for-Food program was nothing more than a corrupt slush fund used by Saddam to build palaces, buy weapons, and buy support from those he could bribe. Hundreds of millions in additional Iraqi oil revenues are simply unaccounted for— and may be sequestered "in trust" by the UN—although this can't be confirmed because auditors have been denied access to the UN's books on the program. Attempts by various media outlets to scrutinize UN financial records have been routinely rebuffed. The UN has no Freedom of Information Act like the one we have in the United States to permit reporters to examine its records and documents.

Despite terror attacks against personnel at its facilities, the UN refuses to take terrorism seriously, and continues to put terrorist nations on a par with peace-loving democracies. In fact, the Blame America First crowd at the UN steadfastly refuses to even define terrorism—perhaps because many UN member nations themselves sponsor terrorism, support it financially, or turn a blind eye to it.

At the UN, this was business as usual. U.S. taxpayers pour billions of dollars each year into the UN coffers and in return get an endless stream of anti-American rhetoric and political posturing from UN bureaucrats and member nations that are virulently opposed to human rights, the rule of law, and democracy. While U.S. forces were toppling Saddam Hussein and rounding up remnants of his regime, the UN was placing Libya in charge of its Human Rights Commission.

The August 19, 2003, terrorist attack on the UN's Baghdad headquarters, which killed top UN envoy Sergio Vieira de Mello and twenty-two others, is instructive. Security was lax because UN officials believe, as "humanitarians," they are immune to terrorism. They put terrorist states on par with peaceful democracies, refuse to condemn terrorism or terrorists, and as was evidenced by the corruption of the UN Oil-for-Food program, chose to work hand-in-glove with a repressive dictator to the detriment of the Iraqi people. Yet the Democrats continue to insist that America's national security and Iraq's future be placed in the hands of this craven and corrupt collection of global bureaucrats.

Turning over command in Iraq to the UN would be tantamount to abandoning our mission, and President Bush has vowed that we will not do that. On the second anniversary of September 11, overseas U.S. troops continued to "carry the fight to the enemy," as President Bush said in his address to the nation. The president reiterated what he told Congress and the country just nine days after those horrific attacks— that the war against terrorism would be fought over a long period of time on many fronts—and then added, "The United States will complete our work in Iraq and Afghanistan." He also predicted that "democracy in those two countries will succeed, and that success will be a great milestone in the history of liberty."

Not long after Saddam was captured, President Bush told members of the New Hampshire Air National Guard, "Terrorists continue to plot and plan against our country...and we must fight this war until our work is done."

CLINTON QUAGMIRE

Yes, we must. It's just a shame that so many Democrats are willing to sacrifice that victory on the altar of politics. Because the worst possible outcome for our country would be a return to the Clinton administration's failed antiterror policies. *Endgame* maps out a strategy that is demanded by the new conditions of the post–September 11 world. But for eight years, Bill Clinton refused to acknowledge the new realities of global Islamic terrorism.

Question for Katie Couric, Peter Jennings, and the gang: Do you *really* want to return to the days of Bill Clinton, when the United States refused to participate in a war that was being foisted upon us?

Well, probably they do. But look at the record. It's easy to forget that Clinton's initiation to the evils of terrorism came early in his tenure. On February 26, 1993, just over a month after his inauguration, Islamic terrorists rented a van, packed it with more than 2,000 pounds of explosives, and parked it in the garage of the World Trade Center. They killed six people and injured more than one thousand.

Their goal? Bring down the building and murder tens of thousands of Americans. President Clinton's response? He wanted to "discourage the American people from overreacting." He never understood the Web of Terror that was being developed worldwide.

Certainly Bill Clinton did not overreact. He turned his attention back to finding a female attorney general without a "nanny problem."

We wound up with Janet Reno. She immediately went to work to teach terrorists a lesson—a lesson in death and destruction. The only problem was that the terrorists in question weren't Osama bin Laden and company, but the Branch Davidians, an offshoot of the Seventh-Day Adventists based in Waco, Texas.

So, in the immediate aftermath of a major terrorist attack on American soil, Bill Clinton's attorney general focused the attention and energies of the FBI, and the Justice Department—not to mention a breathless media elite—on a barn in Waco, where, she said, a crazed cult leader was abusing children. Many questions have been raised in the intervening years about the reliability of the various charges made against the Branch Davidians, and the reasonableness of Reno's reaction. But one thing is certain: the Davidians had never carried out or even contemplated a terrorist attack on American soil.

Eighty people, including twenty-five children, were killed in Reno's fire at Waco. And Americans were not one bit safer from global Islamic terror.

Bill Clinton's response was no better focused when the Murrah Federal Office Building in Oklahoma City was bombed. It wasn't done by radical Muslims, but it showed our vulnerability in a stark fashion. Clinton just blamed it on conservative radio talk show hosts and turned back to defending himself from Whitewater and allegations of other shady dealings. The constant distractions of Whitewater and other such matters kept Clinton from doing much about terrorism in 1995 and 1996—but the terrorists themselves were by no means idle. They carried out attacks that killed twenty-six people and injured nearly 600 in Riyadh on November 13, 1995, and at the Khobar Towers in Saudi Arabia on June 25, 1996.

On August 7, 1998, terrorists attacked U.S. embassies in Nairobi, Kenya, and Dar es Salaam, Tanzania, killing more than 300 and injuring more than 5,000. Then, three days after Mr. Clinton went on national television to finally admit that he did have relations that weren't really sexual with "that woman," he further depleted our precious supply of cruise missiles by attacking a tent camp in Afghanistan and an aspirin factory in Khartoum.

For the next year, while on-again, off-again inspections of Iraqi WMD sites continued, the Clinton administration vacillated between doing nothing to threatening to use force until public opinion polls showed overwhelming opposition to fighting another war in Iraq.

By the summer of 1998, the Clinton administration was deeply embroiled in scandal, and Saddam was able to play the White House like a harp. On August 5, he threw all the UNSCOM (UN Special Commission) inspectors out of Iraq and announced that they would not be allowed back into the country. A few days after this announcement, an Iraqi defector, Khidir Hamza, formerly the head of Saddam's nuclear weapons program, appeared on my radio show. In response to a listener's call, he said, "Saddam will do anything necessary to keep his 'special' weapons. It's all he has to keep him in power. It's too bad this White House doesn't know what needs to be done."

Once again the UN dithered over what to do, and the Clinton administration, by now enmeshed in the Monica Lewinsky affair, deployed U.S. forces to the region—an action that some say was only intended to divert attention from his impeachment proceedings. On December 16, as the U.S. House of Representatives prepared to vote to impeach him, President Clinton launched Operation Desert Fox—a twenty-four-hour-long aerial assault with guided bombs and cruise missiles—aimed at Republican Guard garrisons throughout Iraq. It didn't change a thing. At the end of the day, Bill Clinton was impeached, Saddam Hussein was still in power, and the UNSCOM inspectors never returned to Iraq.

After Operation Desert Fox, the Clinton administration did its best to simply ignore Saddam Hussein. Smarting under criticism from its liberal allies about the cruelty of sanctions, the administration sought to describe the "new" U.S. policy toward Iraq as "containment." It involved little more than U.S. and British aircraft based in Kuwait and Turkey, and aboard carriers in the Persian Gulf, making daily flights over Iraq to enforce expanded no-fly zones. Little or nothing was said or done about Iraq's illicit oil sales, which financed Saddam's WMD program, bribes, and personal enrichment. One U.S. Navy pilot described it to me this way: "Saddam ships oil to Bahrain in the UN Oil-for-Food Program. We buy the oil from the UN and refine it into jet fuel. We put the jet fuel in my F-18 and I go bomb Iraq for violations of UN resolutions. It's nuts."

As the Clinton administration was finally drawing to a close, there came the bombing of the USS *Cole* in Aden, Yemen, on October 12, 2000. Seventeen sailors were killed and thirty-nine others wounded. But Clinton treated the attack more like a bank robbery in Peoria than an act of war against our nation. That would explain why for days after the attack, Secretary of State Madeleine Albright insisted we were "unable to state with certainty that this was a terrorist attack." Madeleine should have called any U.S. Navy sailor. They would have told her.

McINERNEY AND VALLELY:
NO MORE QUAGMIRE

Tom McInerney and Paul Vallely would have, too. They also might have reminded Madeleine—and the congressional Democrats who carry on her outmoded ideals of appeasement and half-measures—about September 11. After that fateful day it is no longer possible for patriotic Americans to be uncertain about the extent or the gravity of the terrorist threat. After September 11 the world changed irrevocably, and old political rivalries and partisan squabbles should have been laid to rest. September 11 called for a new geopolitical vision. Tom McInerney and Paul Vallely have answered that call.

The existence of the global radical Islamic terrorist network threatens this generation and the next. Failure to defeat this network is not an option. But failure is just what we could have if these selfish games continue. McInerney and Vallely aren't interested in relying on the UN or other outmoded and useless institutions. Instead of being wedded to the dead past, they look to the future with confidence and courage. They remind us here that Americans have before, and will in this case, "pay any price and bear any burden" to guarantee the defense of this nation and her people.

We must also ensure that the sacrifices of our soldiers, sailors, airmen, Marines, and first responders are not forgotten. September 11, 2001, changed the world. On that morning, thirty-four-year-old firefighter Stephen Siller had just completed an overnight shift. He was driving to his home on Staten Island when he learned of the attack on the radio. Unable to drive back into Manhattan because of traffic, he was forced to run three miles—with his heavy gear—from the Brooklyn Battery Tunnel to the World Trade Center. Ignoring danger in an attempt to save lives, Siller arrived at the Trade Center and raced into the fire. Minutes later he perished in the first battle of the war on terrorism.

I don't know what firefighter Stephen Siller's politics were, and I don't care. It is long past time to stop seeing the war on terror as a partisan affair. It is, instead, a great challenge for America to respond to new situations with new strategies.

Yet, by mid-February 2004, polls show almost half of Americans think the war in Iraq is a "mistake." Many of the troops still in Iraq tell me that they wonder what kind of reception they will receive when they arrive in America. Some of them shudder at the prospect of a "welcome" like the one their fathers got when they returned from Vietnam. One young Marine wrote: "We won the war. But whether we stay the course to win the peace won't be decided in Baghdad, Basra, or Mosul. That's going to be determined on our television screens, newspapers, and in the corridors of power of Washington. I sure hope we don't leave it up to the media, Hollywood, the UN, or overly ambitious politicians.... I hope they don't snatch defeat from the jaws of victory, like they did with Vietnam."

Rather than doing just that, liberal Democrats and their media allies—along with everyone who loves America—ought to study the insightful analyses and clear thinking displayed by Tom McInerney and Paul Vallely in *Endgame*. It would be good for their mental health, and for the future of our nation.

I have it from the best authority on the planet that Tom and Paul are right about why we fight, why we must win, and what we must do to be victorious. The soldiers, sailors, airmen, guardsmen, and Marines who do the fighting—the warriors of September 11—have told me.

PART ONE

THE FIGHT WE'RE IN

CHAPTER ONE

GETTING TO THE ENDGAME

ODAY, AMERICA IS AT WAR with an enemy every bit as dangerous as Nazi Germany or the Soviet Union: We know it as radical Islam. Like enemies of our past, it draws upon the enforcement of a total ideology that rejects all that is "decadent" about Western liberal democracy. Memories of past glories and promises of their restoration as part of a new golden age fuel this movement that demands unflinching loyalty and ruthlessly stamps out all opposition. It excuses mass murder as necessary and extols the murderers. But it only takes a little investigation to reveal that its promises of liberation are a dubious cover for the blood-spattered tyranny that lies beneath.

If radical Islam were confined to a few benighted countries, we could merely denounce its brutality and celebrate when it was reformed, from afar. But radical Islam's ambitions and reach are global. It does not seek accommodation with its perceived enemies, it is bent solely on their destruction. Radical Islam sees itself locked in a war to the death against the West. To achieve the final victory, it has established a Web of Terror. Using countries where it took hold, such as Iran and Afghanistan, as its bases, radical Islam has established, armed, and funded a large number of terrorist organizations—al-Qaeda, Hezbollah, Palestinian Islamic Jihad, Hamas, and Jemaah Islamiah—that have committed atrocities across the globe. Drawing on the oil wealth of Saudi Arabia, radical clerics have established mosques and religious schools around the world that spread a militant, inflexible, and intolerant version of Islam, serve as centers of recruitment for terrorist organizations, and raise financial support for those organizations. The Web of Terror's number-one enemy—and thus its number-one target—is the United States, because without the sword and shield provided by the U.S. military, the rest of the West will have no choice but to submit.

It has been widely reported that Osama bin Laden saw America's tepid reaction to terrorist acts against it in the 1980s and the 1990s as proof that the United States no longer had the will to protect itself. He reasoned that one spectacular blow at the symbols of American power would be enough to bring our country to its knees and make the world capitulate to his dreams of a new Islamic empire. Fortunately, the Bush administration was different from the Clinton administration; it accepted that the United States was in a war and did not try to minimize the terrorist acts as a law enforcement problem. Because President Bush decided to deal with the Web of Terror forthrightly and was unafraid to use American power—in its many forms—within two years of the attacks of September 11, 2001, the United States and its allies have overthrown two of the most important regimes within the Web of Terror.

But the war is not over. The prospect of a free and democratic Iraq and Afghanistan is threatened by the Islamists who would return these countries to tyranny. Syria allows jihadists to flow into Iraq to fight the coalition forces and disrupt Iraqi society. The Iranian regime is training and supporting terrorists, including those attacking our soldiers in Iraq, and is working feverishly to develop nuclear weapons. Iran's efforts to develop nuclear weapons has been advanced by Pakistani nuclear scientists and Saudi Arabian petro-dollars as well as support from the ultimate rogue state, North Korea. Iran will probably have a nuclear weapon within six to twelve months.

In North Korea, the dictator Kim Jong Il has impoverished his country and starved his people in order to build nuclear weapons and guided missiles—technologies he will certainly sell to radical Muslims with whom he has made common cause.

Post–September 11, the members of the Web of Terror have realized that America is more resilient than they thought. Therefore, its plans have grown more dramatic. We fear—and that is the correct word—that the next major terrorist attack on the United States will be conducted with weapons of mass destruction, particularly nuclear weapons. That is why we must act now to destroy the terror masters before they can strike us.

Our book is meant to provide a blueprint for victory, an endgame that will eliminate the Web of Terror. We speak not as armchair generals, but as retired generals of the Air Force and the Army who have devoted the bulk of our lives to defending the United States. We speak also as military analysts for FOX News Channel, positions that have allowed us to keep up-to-the-minute with all that is occurring in the Pentagon, the CIA, and elsewhere in the U.S. government related to the war on terrorism.

We also know the men and women on "the sharp edge" of the war on terror, in the rifle companies, artillery batteries, tank platoons, Special Operating Forces, bomber wings, airlift squadrons, communications detachments, fighter squadrons, aircraft carriers, submarines, cruisers, destroyers, and amphibious warfare ships. These are the people who do the fighting, the "peacekeeping," and, inevitably, the dying. These active-duty National Guard and Reserve soldiers, sailors, airmen, Marines, and coast guard are the best this nation has to offer.

During a visit we made to Baghdad in 2003, a young soldier told us that the war on terror cannot be lost on the battlefield; but it can be lost if the will of the American people falters: they must understand why we fight. This book is our attempt to explain not only why we fight, but how we will win.

Lt. General Tom McInerney writes as an expert on high-tech warfare who served for thirty-five years in the U.S. Air Force. Tom was a career fighter pilot who served four tours in Vietnam, commanded a numbered air force during a major strike against a terrorist country, and was a joint force commander (his command was composed of the 6th Infantry Division [Light] and the 11th Air Force and was supported by the Navy's Third Fleet). His final assignment was as the assistant vice chief of staff of the U.S. Air Force and director of the Defense Performance Review, reporting directly to the secretary of defense. Maj. General Paul Vallely writes as an expert on special operations, psychological/information warfare, and civil-military operations. Like Tom, he is a graduate of West Point. In fact, we were at West Point together—Tom started life as an infantry officer before transferring to the Air Force—but we never crossed paths again, despite serving in Vietnam at the same time, until FOX News Channel brought us together as military analysts after September 11. Paul served in the Army for thirty-two years, seeing two combat tours in Vietnam and duty around the world before retiring as deputy commanding general, U.S. Army, Pacific. As military analysts at FOX News Channel, we developed the network's "war room." More important, we were recognized as the military analysts who got things right more often than anyone else in the popular media. In part that was because of our sources, and in part it was because we based our analysis on fact, not spin, and what we knew of the United States military's capabilities, not on the hopes or fears or on what other commentators were saying. In this book, our intention is to offer the same kind of analysis—factual, doable, realistic.

KNOW YOUR ENEMY

The first step in confronting our enemy is to know it, define it, and deal with it. The Web of Terror is made up of eight terror-sponsoring countries. The qualifications to be a Web of Terror nation are that it supports and/or sponsors terrorism and is involved with weapons of mass destruction. Without the support of these countries, terrorist groups like al-Qaeda would not be a serious threat. Our mission is to defeat al-Qaeda by defeating the Web of Terror. In other words, they have a choice to take a path of cooperation or a path of defiance. That means changing, or achieving major policy shifts in, six of the regimes that make up the Web of Terror, and helping guide the other two on a path of political reform. The six are Afghanistan, Iraq, Iran, Syria, North Korea, and Libya. Of these six regimes, the United States has forcibly changed two already. Afghanistan was the nest of the Taliban and al-Qaeda. It no longer is. Saddam Hussein's Iraq was in many ways the center of gravity of the Web of Terror. It was central geographically, bordering Syria, Iran, and Saudi Arabia. It was central in its contempt for the West with its daily violations of UN resolutions, firing on British and American aircraft, and continuation of WMD research and development. It was central in that it had produced and used WMDs in the past. And it was central because it was a way-station for terrorists who could contact scientists working on WMD research, something that America's former weapons inspector David Kay not only affirmed but said was more likely than we ever realized. The Hussein regime had already once tried to assassinate a former American president—George H. W. Bush. Certainly, it would have had few compunctions about giving ricin, anthrax, or some other poisonous agent to a terrorist group for a strike against the United States, if Iraq could maintain plausible deniability.

Of the remaining regimes:

Libya today shows signs of reform, as Muammar Gaddafi has observed America's liberation of Iraq and taken the obvious clue. He has abandoned his quest for nuclear weapons, surrendered his research facilities, and is trying to reach something of an accommodation with the West.

Syria continues its role as a major terrorist sponsor—and according to reliable intelligence, which we have reported on FOX News Channel, may be the hiding place of Iraqi WMDs, along with the Bekaa Valley in Lebanon. But for all the trouble it causes in the region, for all the terrorism it sponsors, Syria is a paper tiger that could fold if enough pressure is applied.

Iran is a great danger because of its rush to build a nuclear weapon and because it is the heart of the Web of Terror. President Jimmy Carter's decision to let the Shah of Iran fall was a monumental one. In a sense, the Ayatollah Khomeini was the spider that spun the Web of Terror. Iran, until 1979, had been a moderately Western-oriented country and an ally to the United States. After the revolution of 1978–1979, it became the nation where a revolutionary Islamic fundamentalist state was first established. As such it provided other radical Islamists with an encouraging example that even the most apparently resilient regime could be overthrown by a dedicated cadre of activists and that a forthrightly Islamic regime could be established in its stead and enjoy broad popular support (for a time, at least). Under the control of those who toppled the Shah, Iran also became a leading exporter of radical Islam and a leading supporter of Islamist terrorism. Some analysts also have stated that the rise of a Shi'ite Islamic state in Iran spurred the House of Saud to expand its efforts to spread its ascetic Wahabbi theology, which has spawned a large number of problems. Now, however, the open and growing domestic opposition to Iran's despotic mullahs is bringing the political situation in Iran to the point where regime change might be easier to accomplish in Iran than it was in Iraq.

The last country is the Web of Terror's one non-Islamic component, North Korea. Too many policymakers take the position that there is very little we can do to reform North Korea, because we can bring no viable military pressure to bear on it, given North Korea's fanatically militarized regime. That argument is false, and later in the book we will show why.

The two regimes that need reforming are Saudi Arabia, whose enormous standing and financial resources in the Islamic world have been used to promote the Web of Terror—often in ways contrary to the kingdom's own interests. The other regime is Pakistan, which has a record of advancing radical Islamist groups through official and quasi-official means. Pakistan's current president, Pervez Musharraf, has shown immense bravery and no lack of nerve in confronting his country's rogue nuclear scientists and trying to tame the Islamists in Pakistan's political and military establishments. More work, however, needs to be done to ensure that Pakistan is a firm partner in the war against terrorism.

Change the regimes in these countries, or reform them, and the Web of Terror withers away—and that includes al-Qaeda and the "subsidiaries" in its terror conglomerate. Countering al-Qaeda's terrorism as a police matter will not end it. Focusing solely on al-Qaeda's amorphous network and not on the rogue states that give it sustenance will not destroy it. The Web of Terror nurtured and supported al-Qaeda and its related organizations. Destroy the Web of Terror and al-Qaeda is destroyed and with it, the chief threat to America's security today: weapons of mass destruction in the hands of terrorists.

Any other solution is incomplete—and, by being incomplete, dangerous. The scenarios if we don't act are frightening, which only underlines why they must be avoided. It's time to consider them now.

CHAPTER TWO

THE NIGHTMARES

OUR ENEMY, THE RADICAL Islamists, dream of resurrecting the great Muslim empire that once spanned the Middle East, North Africa, the Balkans, and parts of Central Asia, and of establishing an Islamic super-state that stretches from Malaysia's border with Thailand through Indonesia, the largest Muslim country in the world, to the southern Philippines. They even foresee an Islamic conquest of Europe, through the influence of radical mullahs in European mosques, through the infiltration of radical Islamist terrorist cells into Western countries, and through the demographic growth of Islamic populations versus the declining populations of secular or Christian Europe. Their dream is to create a global empire with the likes of Osama bin Laden or the Taliban's former leader Mullah Omar at its head. The Islamists' dream is the West's nightmare.

But even if the radical Islamists' dream is overblown, they and their Stalinist cohort, North Korea, could nevertheless present the United States with several nightmare scenarios. Here they are, in rising levels of importance.

THE LEBANONIZATION OF IRAQ

Until the late 1960s, Israel's and Syria's neighbor, Lebanon, though never entirely free from strife, was known for its relative stability, peace, and prosperity. Set on the Mediterranean Sea, its capital Beirut was a great trading city—and European holiday destination—renowned for its beauty and sophistication. All that changed after Lebanon was caught literally in the crossfire of the Arab-Israeli dispute, which caused Lebanon's own religious divisions to boil over into civil war and chaos.

Today, although Beirut is being slowly rebuilt, Syria still occupies and dominates Lebanon. The Syrian presence means that Lebanon must tolerate the presence of terrorist groups, especially the Palestinian Islamic Jihad, Hamas, Yasser Arafat's al-Fatah, Iran's Revolutionary Guard Corps, and the Iranian-supported Hezbollah, the yellow flag of which flies some ten yards from the UN flag, as we saw when we visited the Israel-Lebanon border near Metulla. It is deplorable that the UN permits such a display.

Turning Iraq, with its rich oil and gas fields, into another Lebanon— that is, a state where a foreign power dominates the country and turns it to terrorist ends—is a major goal of the Web of Terror and especially of the Iranian government.

Iraq's strategic position is crucial to the Middle East, with a port on the Persian Gulf, and borders with Iran, Turkey, Syria, Kuwait, and Jordan. Make Iraq an ally of the West, bordering such moderate Islamic states as Kuwait, Turkey, and Jordan, and you create a much more hopeful future for the region. Let it fall prey to the mullahs of Iran, and suddenly radical Islam has a new base sitting on vast oil fields.

Lebanon was home to many different ethnic and religious groups— Sunni, Shi'ite, Maronite Christian (many of whom were driven out of the country), and Druze. Iraq, too, is home to many different ethnic and religious groups—Sunni, Shi'ite, Kurds, Turkmen, and a small but historic minority of Christians. As Lebanon was largely a creation of the French Republic after World War I, Iraq was a creation of the British Empire. Now, the glue that held the country together since 1958, the national socialist Ba'ath Party, which adhered to the 1950s-vintage ideology of "Arab nationalism" is gone. Iran and Syria would like nothing better than to tear Iraq apart and then grab what they can of it. That's what makes our continued presence vital to the long-term stability of Iraq and the region: if we stabilize Iraq and help it develop an Arab version of democracy, it will mark a major advance against the Web of Terror.

ı   ı   ı   ı   ı   ı   ı   ı   ı

There are two obvious vehicles for Islamist subversion in Iraq. One is for radical clerics, sponsored by Iran or Saudi Arabia, to infiltrate Iraqi mosques and religious schools. The other is for the Iranians to send terrorists, spies, and fighters into the country and for other countries—for example, the Saudis—to allow them into Iraq. By the summer of 2003, it became obvious that the Iranian intelligence agents already had infiltrated Shi'ite areas of Iraq, hoping to cause disaffection. The Iranians—who have already sent tons of arms to the PLO and Hezbollah in Palestine and Lebanon—might also try sending weapons, ammunition, and other equipment to those among Iraq's Shi'ite population who support the goals of the Iranian mullahs. Before Iraq's liberation, Iran harbored a core of Iraqi exiles armed for resistance to Saddam Hussein. It would be easy, therefore, for the Iranians to deploy a serious proxy force against U.S. troops and against those Iraqis, Shi'ite and otherwise, who support true democracy rather than an Iranian-style theocracy.

All that is necessary for Iran's plans in Iraq to succeed is for Iraq's political development to be disrupted. Most Iraqis are excited and hopeful about their imminent democratic self-government. Think of the corrosive effect, however, if a political faction, ethnic group, or religious sect dominates the new Iraqi government or if cronyism and corruption seep into it, or if it is inefficient and ineffectual, or, most important, if it cannot provide security against crime, terrorism, and external threats.

Obviously, for the Iranians, the Syrians, and the radical Islamists, concerted programs of subversion, propaganda, assassination, and sabotage against Iraq's new government will be a priority. Their goal: turn Iraq into a latter-day Lebanon, a country embroiled in a brutal civil war of rival militias, and then pry it apart. There are three geographical levers with which they could attempt to achieve the goal. In the north, if the Kurds tried to secede, Iran and Turkey might intervene militarily on the pretense of protecting themselves from their own restive Kurdish minorities. If Iran stripped off southern Iraq as a Shi'ite Republic, it would become an annex of the most dangerous Islamist regime on the planet. If the Sunni rump of central Iraq were left to extremists—and the most extreme form of Islam, Wahhabism, is based in Sunni Islam—it could become a new Taliban-like state and a base for groups like al-Qaeda. What will stop all of this from happening is an American political commitment to put Iraq on its feet politically and economically and support it militarily until it can support itself.

CHANGE FOR THE DEVIL WE KNOW:
THE HOUSE OF SAUD

Some people would not shed a tear if the Saudi royal family disappeared overnight. Elements of the Saudi government have been "enablers" of Islamic radicalism. At home, the House of Saud is strictly repressive. It is regarded as an ally of the United States—but on its own terms, which only recently, only after the Saudis themselves were hit, have begun to include discouraging terrorism. Our concern with the House of Saud is tempered, however, by the realization that whatever and whoever replaced its hundreds of princes could be much worse than they have been, are, and might be.

Until May 2003, the House of Saud's grip on its country looked firm. But an informed analyst will tell you that only one in four Saudi subjects—the technocrats, military officers, diplomats, and businessmen who have been educated in, or have extensive dealings with, the West—is unflinchingly loyal to the House of Saud. The other three-quarters of the Saudi population view the ruling house and its denizens as hypocrites who fund mosques, religious schools, and Islamic universities and are the custodians of Islam's two holiest sites, Mecca and Medina. They see them as both corrupt—running the country exclusively in their own interest—and corrupted by the forbidden pleasures of the West.

Some, including many members of the royal family, argue that the House of Saud would gain popularity if it created a written, democratic constitution (it currently asserts that its constitution is the Koran) and held elections. On the other hand, many analysts predict that any democratic elections would make Osama bin Laden, or his equivalent, prime minister of Saudi Arabia.

While some constitutional reform is possible, the reality is that the House of Saud is in a showdown with the radical Islamists. In this fight, the House of Saud would seem to have the upper hand, with an extensive and effective internal security apparatus and control of the nation's religious establishment. Moreover, the House of Saud has not one but two guard units drawn from the Sauds' own tribe and separate from the army—the Royal Guard Battalion and the larger Saudi Arabian National Guard—that will loyally defend the regime.

While this offers some reassurance, the example of the Shah of Iran should be instructive to the Saudi royal family. The Shah had a large and dreaded secret police—SAVAK—and an Imperial Guard consisting of two well-equipped divisions. As impressive as they were, both the Shah's police apparatus and the Imperial Guard were not enough to overcome Iran's popular Islamist revolution. Reports that Islamists have penetrated the Saudi military and police as well as other government institutions now surface with disturbing regularity. All of this raises the nightmare scenario of the fall of Saudi Arabia and the establishment of the Islamic Republic of Arabia and of a state as radical as Afghanistan under the Taliban, but incomparably wealthier.

Consider what al-Qaeda was able to accomplish when it was headquartered in two wretchedly poor nations, Sudan and Afghanistan:

the bombings of American embassies in Africa, the development of a worldwide terror network, the bombing of the USS *Cole*, and the attacks on September 11, 2001. Now think what al-Qaeda could do with full access to Saudi Arabia's petro-dollars and relatively well-developed infrastructure. Islamist terrorists from Indonesia, the Philippines, Nigeria, and elsewhere would travel to Saudi Arabia; meet with the heads of the Arabian Republic's intelligence and security services; and ask for money, weapons, manpower, training centers, and transport to attack Western interests and moderate Muslims. Then there is the specter of what analysts call Saudi Arabia's "oil weapon." An Islamist Saudi Arabia could cripple the economies of the United States, Europe, and even Japan simply by shutting off the flow of oil. In his book on U.S.-Saudi relations, *Sleeping with the Devil*, former CIA officer Robert Baer estimates that in such a scenario the price of oil could skyrocket to $150 a barrel. If the Arabian Republic were able to intimidate the ruling families of the relatively small Gulf States, the price could go even higher. Unlike the monarchs who rule Saudi Arabia and the Gulf States, Islamist revolutionaries believe in destroying the West, not necessarily trading with the West; they would have no compunction about devastating Western economies even at the cost of hundreds of billions of dollars in lost revenue. They also could use the oil weapon to divide the West by holding out the prospect of a renewed flow of oil in exchange for pro-Islamist policies of appeasement, effectively turning some Western governments, desperate to do just about anything to keep the oil flowing, into de facto allies against the United States and its partners.

NUCLEAR NIGHTMARE I: NORTH KOREA'S SUICIDE

In early October 2003, North Korea announced that, through the reprocessing of spent nuclear fuel rods, it had enough plutonium to begin the production of nuclear weapons. Some dismiss this as typical North Korean braggadocio or the opening move in an attempt to shake down the Americans, Chinese, and Russians for the fuel, food, and other support needed to prop up the North Korean regime. However, based on the fact that North Korea has not only poured huge amounts of money and manpower into developing nuclear weapons, but has also assisted Iran's efforts to build nuclear weapons, we think that these threats must be taken seriously.

I I I I I I I I I

If North Korea has built operational nuclear weapons—and it probably has—there is no doubt that Japan would seriously consider developing its own nuclear deterrent. Even South Korea could embark on a program to get its own weapons—it has the technology, and much better financial resources than North Korea.

But a "nuclearized" Northeast Asia is not our main concern. We think that the North Korean regime considers nuclear weapons as the key to its conquest of South Korea. It could brandish nuclear weapons at Japan and the United States (the latter if it manages to complete the development of long-range ICBMs), threatening to use them against these countries if they dare come to South Korea's defense. Essentially, the North Koreans would pose a question to the United States and Japan: Respectively, are you willing to put Honolulu, Anchorage, and Seattle and Tokyo, Kyoto, and Yokohama at risk of nuclear annihilation in order to defend Seoul and Pusan? North Korea thinks the answer is no. We think the answer is yes. The real answer, however, is to prevent North Korea from acquiring nuclear weapons in the first place.

NUCLEAR NIGHTMARE II: IRAN

We think most analysts are unaware of how close the Iranians might be to producing an operational nuclear weapon. In fact, Iran's crash nuclear program could produce a weapon at any moment. Whether

Iran has nuclear weapons in a month's time or a year's time, we must consider what the mullahs will do with them once they have them. Would they be used solely as a deterrent against Israel? To raise the prestige of the mullahs' regime in the Islamic world (the *second* "Islamic bomb")? Or would they be used to fulfill the mullahs' regional and global ambitions?

Unfortunately, based on Iran's past record as an active promoter of Islamic revolution and terrorism, it seems likely that if Iran acquired nuclear weapons, they would be used to advance the mullahs' radical agenda for the Middle East and the world.

One likely scenario is that Iran would use its nuclear weapons or sale of a North Korean nuclear weapon to terrorists to "solve" the Palestinian question to its satisfaction. Among Palestinians—especially the younger ones who have no memory of the PLO's former status as the darling of many Arab countries—Yasser Arafat's corrupt Palestinian Authority is losing popularity to the Iranian-supported Islamist Palestinian nationalist groups, Hamas and Palestinian Islamic Jihad. Moreover, the seventy-four-year-old Yasser Arafat is in declining health, with reports alleging that he suffers from a variety of ailments ranging from Parkinson's disease, to stomach cancer, to cardiac problems. Protective of his power, Arafat has anointed no successor, and his own paranoia about threats to this power has led him to establish numerous military groups, all of which report to him but none of which is big enough to overthrow him. If brought together by their Iranian sponsors or placed under the "temporary" command of Iranian Revolutionary Guard cadres, Hamas and Palestinian Islamic Jihad would have two major advantages over the Palestinian Authority's competing military elements—unity of command and unity of purpose.

Another Iranian proxy, Hezbollah, already is in a strong position in southern Lebanon. If Hamas and Palestinian Islamic Jihad seized control of the West Bank and Gaza Strip, these groups would have the ability to combine the areas under their control and proclaim them the Islamic Republic of Palestine. Their likely next course would be exterminating or exiling all of their internal enemies, and then unleashing a massive terror campaign against Israeli settlements on the West Bank and in Jerusalem, as well as launching attacks on Israel from Gaza and southern Lebanon. Iran, of course, would recognize the new Palestinian state and declare that any attack against it would be met with a nuclear response from Iran. Israel would face the choice of nuclear war with Iran or accommodation with an Islamist Palestine on Iran's terms. Given that these terms would probably be draconian—the elimination of Israel as a state—Israel and Iran could very well fight the first nuclear war in history.

NUCLEAR NIGHTMARE III:
ANOTHER SEPTEMBER 11

Last fall, we learned that the initial plan for the September 11, 2001, attacks was to use ten airliners—five on the East Coast, five on the West Coast—as flying bombs. The deaths of more than three thousand people in the Pentagon, the World Trade Center, and Pennsylvania notwithstanding, the terrorists did not manage to inflict much long-term damage through their September 11 attacks. Commerce, air travel, and the financial markets quickly resumed, the federal government was fully functional, and the United States did not abandon its allies in the Middle East. We can only suppose, therefore, that if terrorists were to strike us again they would want to strike a truly devastating blow.

Our nightmare—made more nightmarish because it is so plausible—is that the next strike would consist of the simultaneous detonation of multiple nuclear weapons in many major cities in the United States such as New York, Washington, Detroit, Seattle, Los Angeles, Chicago, Atlanta, Houston, New Orleans, and Miami.

Getting the bombs or the components for the bombs into the United States would be simple. They are relatively small and easily concealed in larger cargo or in a shipping container. Smuggling them into the United States would not be difficult because, despite the steps taken after September 11, 2001, our borders remain inexcusably porous. If the price was right, the criminal gangs that currently move illegal narcotics and immigrants into this country would help smuggle nuclear weapons and/or nuclear materials over our borders. The bombs would not have to be huge "city busters." Weapons with even the relatively small yield of twenty kilotons and exploded on the ground (nuclear weapons exploded in the air are more destructive) would produce catastrophic results in the target cities.

Hundreds of thousands of Americans would be killed immediately; many more would be horridly wounded, a large number, mortally. Millions more would be consigned to a lifetime of worry about the effects of radiation poisoning on them and their families. Beyond the appalling human cost, there would be grave damage to the country's ability to govern itself, to function as a coherent economic unit, to communicate internally, to rebuild our cities, to aid our allies, and to strike back at our enemies. If the bomb meant for Washington were set off in front of the Library of Congress, it would destroy the Capitol and the Supreme Court, pulverize many government offices, including the Department of Health and Human Services (which has many crucial emergency functions), and kill thousands of people vital to the proper functioning of government—cabinet secretaries, civil servants, senators, and congressmen. If they survived the attack, the president, the vice president, and their staffs would move to a safe location, as would the surviving officials of any government departments fortunate enough to have headquarters a safe distance from Ground Zero. At once, the country's capital would be heavily damaged and largely abandoned by the government.

A bomb in midtown Manhattan would effectively wipe out important financial, corporate, and cultural institutions as well as destroy the headquarters of many of America's news media outlets and punch a mammoth hole in the heart of America's greatest city. The cities of Los Angeles and Miami are economic and financial gateways to the Pacific Rim and Latin America, respectively. Attacks on these cities, therefore, would not only damage the American economy but also have ripple effects far beyond the borders of the United States.

Of course, economic recovery would be the farthest thing from the minds of most Americans who would be dealing with the immediate effects of the attacks. Even in those cities not directly affected by the attacks, there probably would be damage to and disruption of electrical power, transportation, and communications systems. Unless it was immediately known that some form of federal executive authority was still in place—albeit not in Washington—there would be concerns about authority and coordination of recovery, military response, and security efforts. There might not be much, if any, knowledge of the true nature of the attack and its scope for days, maybe even weeks.

Once Americans understood *what* had happened, we still would not know exactly *how* it happened or *who* conducted the strike. Unlike the investigators of the Oklahoma City bombing, investigators would not find pieces of trucks that they could trace to rental agencies and to the bombers. Evidence would vaporize as part of the ultimate suicide bombing. Even more important, there would be a gnawing fear: Are there more weapons out there? Could there be other attacks on other American cities? Could other terror cells strike the cities already attacked?

If, after some time, we discovered that, say, al-Qaeda was the culprit, what would our reaction be? Would we invade the country where the terrorists have their headquarters? What if the headquarters are in Riyadh, Jakarta, or Islamabad? Would we issue a request for extradition? If intelligence revealed that Iran had a hand in the strike, how would we respond? Would we stay our hand from total retaliation out of concern for the millions of truly innocent Iranians behind whom the mullahs would be hiding?

No matter how we decided to respond, there is no guarantee that our allies would support us in that response. Knowing that nuclear weapons could be in their major cities, they could declare themselves neutral and deny us any support, material or otherwise. If those who attacked us seized that moment to attack Israel, the Europeans might turn a blind eye to the situation and a deaf ear to pleas for help from Jerusalem. Whatever else you might say about the Israelis, when it comes to survival, they do not shrink from the task. Israel could decide to mount a preemptive strike against Iran.

Many of the scenarios about terrorism concern "weapons of mass destruction," otherwise known as nuclear, chemical, and biological weapons. There is ample reason to believe that these weapons are in the arsenals of some Web of Terror nations or soon will be. Knowing these weapons' terrible effects, we should be deeply concerned about the threat they pose to this country and our allies. As grave as the threats posed by biological and chemical weapons are, however, they are not as grave as that posed by nuclear weapons. As the SARS crisis of 2002–2003 showed, even when facing a heretofore-unknown disease, steps to arrest or at least retard the spread of the disease can be taken. We are relatively well prepared against biological attacks, and their impact would likely be limited. A biological attack would not destroy the infrastructure that our country depends on. Telephone lines would be working. Electricity would be generated and transmitted. Highways and railroads would remain open. Computer networks would remain functioning. However frightening a biological attack might be in theory, it is unlikely to achieve much in fact.

Both of us served in Germany during the Cold War, and the threat from the massive Soviet chemical arsenal was never far from our minds—and with good reason. Chemical weapons' effects are gruesome and, depending on the particular agent, the dose needed to kill or severely injure can be small. Nevertheless, delivering these weapons in a manner and quantity that would be sure to cause massive casualties would be no easy matter. These weapons are just as deadly to the attacker as to the target and so demand careful handling. Even if a terrorist group were given chemical weapons from the arsenal of a country, there is no guarantee that they would be able to transport them safely to the target cities or gather them in sufficient quantities to kill and injure large numbers of people.

Most chemical weapons lose their effectiveness over time as wind, sun, and rain dissipate and dilute them. Moreover, there are proven, effective means to counter these weapons, contain their effects, and prevent casualties from mounting. And chemical weapons, like biological weapons, do not destroy buildings or bridges or any other vital infrastructure or interfere seriously in the operation of government.

From a military perspective, therefore, using nuclear weapons just makes more sense. Mounting a terrorist operation using weapons of mass destruction would be expensive, even if the most expensive item—the weapons themselves—were "donated" by Iran or North Korea. It would be extremely wasteful for the Web of Terror to expend immense amounts of time, money, and manpower on an operation that would *not* deliver a crushing blow to the United States.

Given the current crash weapons programs of Iran and North Korea and the questionable security of weapons under the control of Pakistan and Russia, a terrorist nuclear strike against the United States is more than possible. It is very likely. Preventing such an attack by arresting the proliferation of nuclear weapons among the members of the Web of Terror, therefore, must be of paramount concern for America's president.

NUCLEAR NIGHTMARE IV: REVENGE

In the immediate aftermath of the September 11 attacks, there was concern that the United States would retaliate in a way that one person described as "Going Roman"—the utter destruction of the sponsors of the terrorists who killed thousands of our citizens. Would the United States do to, say, Afghanistan what Rome did to Carthage? As events proved, the United States is not cast in the Roman mold; President Bush did not take the approach that characterizes so much of human history and launch a campaign of extermination in Afghanistan. Our campaign against the Taliban and al-Qaeda was a model of restraint. It would have been a far simpler matter to attack Kabul and Kandahar from the air in hopes of pummeling the Taliban into submission and smashing al-Qaeda into atoms—as the U.S. Air Force's circling B-52s were quite capable of doing. Instead of destroying entire villages or large patches of Kabul, however, our commanders used our air power with more care and precision than in any previous war. Certainly, a country bent on exacting revenge and sowing fear would not have bothered to try to avoid hitting mosques, schools, and hospitals, as we did.

In Iraq, the fear of many—and apparent desire of some—was that Baghdad would be reduced to rubble, with American artillery and air power pulverizing the city, block by block. If that had been done, thousands of civilians would have been killed and wounded and many thousands more would have been made homeless. In stark contrast to the fears and dreams of some, the cities, towns, and villages of Iraq were left essentially intact, and far fewer Iraqis were killed or injured in the weeks of fighting in Operation Iraqi Freedom than the critics of the campaign had predicted with such utter certainty. It is important to note as well that the stated mission of the Iraqi campaign was not the subjugation of the Iraqi people, the destruction of Iraq's national identity, or the eradication of Iraqi culture. Quite the contrary, the campaign was about ousting a dictator who sponsored terrorism, pursued (and had used in the past) weapons of mass destruction, enslaved the Iraqi people, and bent Iraq's national identity and culture to his own ends. But if nuclear weapons are exploded on American soil, such carefully measured responses would not do. In response, the American president would indeed "Go Roman." The instruments of counterstrike are on the tips of missiles in silos and on board submarines, ready for immediate launch. In the absence of absolute evidence pinpointing the source of such nuclear terror—and given that the Web of Terror is international in scope—the American government would still know that the nuclear bombs used could have come from only a limited number of countries. The most likely suspects would be Pakistan, Iran, and North Korea. And the money to fund such a bold operation would have come from a limited list of donors—most probably, Iran or Saudi Arabia. Teasing out the details of the plot would be left for later. International and domestic calls for restraint and warnings about "the Arab Street" would be irrelevant. Nuclear retaliation against Tehran, Pyongyang, and the capital of any other suspected regime would be a given.

If you don't think this scenario is likely then you have a higher opinion of human nature than we do. With many of our major cities shattered and millions of Americans dead or dying, an American president who did not retaliate in kind would not long remain president. The repercussions of American retaliation would be profound: the deaths of perhaps tens of millions, the shock and distrust of our allies, and a dividing line in domestic politics as stark as that of the Civil War.

We present this scenario as a warning of the consequences of inaction and appeasement against the Web of Terror. If we act now, revenge will not be necessary, because we can destroy the Web of Terror using less destructive strategies and tactics, such as we will outline in this book. The alternative is to sit back, trust in the good intentions of those regimes whose stated goal is our destruction, and be left with revenge as our only option.

We present this scenario of massive retaliation by the United States for another reason. Our enemies, and any supposed ally who would betray us, should know the risks they run. Critics might call it "cowboy justice." They might call it "international vigilantism." They might even call it "mass murder." But it is what would happen. Whoever attacked the United States in such a manner or assisted in any such attack against the United States would be utterly destroyed, their countries made radioactive wastelands. Our country could retaliate without breaking a sweat. One Trident missile submarine could do the job in sixty minutes, tops. Do we take a perverse pleasure in the prospect of so massive an American response? Far from it. As men who know what these weapons mean, this is a nightmare we want to avoid; avoiding it is a reason we wrote this book.

Some have said that the war on terror could last twenty-five, fifty, a hundred years. We cannot wait that long. We need to defeat the Web of Terror now, not just deter it for some indefinite period, hoping it runs out of gas or that time will somehow heal the perceived wounds that drive those who want us destroyed. State sponsors of terrorism must destroy the monsters they have created—or they themselves will be destroyed. Saudi Arabia and Pakistan must clean their own nests, while Iran, North Korea, Syria, and Libya either must change regimes, or, as Libya has professed to do, cease supporting terror and surrender any ambitions to develop weapons of mass destruction. As we will show, we can make that choice even simpler for them.

PART TWO

HOW WE FIGHT

CHAPTER THREE

NEW CAMPAIGNS, NEW STRATEGIES

T WOULD BE FOLLY FOR the United States and its allies to wait for the results of the 2004 presidential and congressional elections before they lay out a comprehensive strategy against the Web of Terror. The terrorists will not wait until January 20, 2005, and neither should we.

Our grand strategic goal is quite simple: to ensure the security of the United States by thoroughly defeating the Web of Terror. That means drying up the sources of weapons, funding, and manpower for terrorist groups, and denying them territorial sanctuaries. It means stopping nuclear proliferation and dismantling the WMD development programs and weapons stockpiles of rogue states. It means encouraging the spread of democracy in the Muslim world. And it means resolving the Palestinian question in a fair and equitable manner between two democratic entities—the State of Israel and a *reformed* Palestinian Authority.

We cannot wait to achieve these goals or expect that these changes will happen of their own volition. In some cases, achieving these goals will mean overthrowing regimes, as we did with the Taliban and Saddam Hussein, though the means by which we do so might vary. A case in point could be Iran. Even if Iran officially ends its nuclear weapons development program, it is doubtful that the mullahs will cease arming, training, and funding terror groups around the world. The only serious question remaining, therefore, is how to achieve regime change in Iran, and whether that will be done through support for the growing domestic resistance to the mullahs, diplomatic pressure, military force, or some combination of the three. In other cases, we will have to engage in *regime preservation*, helping governments secure themselves against Islamist violence so that eventual democratic reform is possible. Nuclear-armed Pakistan, for example, could fall to an Islamist military coup or become a bloody battleground between religious sects, secularists, and foreign jihadists. Pakistan's government, for the long-term benefit of all (except the jihadists), needs democratic reform, but not before it neutralizes the domestic Islamist threat.

The first key concept is the need to press at utmost speed the war on terror to achieve regime change throughout the Web of Terror—supporting states. Another key concept is preemption. President Bush was right to make this a strategic principle of his administration. Preemption's purpose is to put teeth behind the idea that certain actions are utterly unacceptable. Thumb your nose at UN weapons inspectors, and the United States will not risk that it can trust you; it will, in fact, enforce UN threats that the UN itself won't enforce. Sell or transfer nuclear weapons and their delivery systems—cruise missiles and ICBMs—to rogue states or terrorist groups, and America will stop you, by force if necessary. It would be folly to let inaction lead to nuclear proliferation, to wait until a nuclear weapon falls into the hands of al-Qaeda or detonates in New York or London, before we act in our own defense.

Another key concept is simultaneity. We simply do not have the time to take a sequential approach: first Afghanistan, then Iraq, perhaps next North Korea, and so on. Every strand in the Web of Terror needs to be snipped—now. Thankfully, work *is* being done on many fronts. However, it is not enough and it is not being done anywhere near fast enough. What follows next are the campaigns that must be won.

Afghanistan

The key to achieving lasting success in Afghanistan is establishing its security. As the country's interim president, Hamid Karzai, admitted when he addressed the British Labour Party's annual conference in October 2003, less than half the country is under the rule of law. Though the Afghans have a completed constitution, plans for democratic elections, and an education system again open to women, the establishment of a fully functioning civil society is *years* in the future. According to some estimates, there are 100,000 fighters under the command of provincial leaders and regional warlords—and rivalries between them remain strong. The followers of these leaders and warlords don't just have AK-47 assault rifles, they have tanks, armored personnel carriers, and heavy artillery—and some of these weapons are placed near Kabul.

To defuse this volatile situation, President Karzai included a section in the Law of Political Parties, decreed in the fall of 2003, stating that political parties could not have military organizations affiliated with them. In addition, he was able to negotiate an agreement among the militias and other armed factions to abide by the terms of the United Nations' disarmament plan.

This is fine on paper, but for the disarmament plan to make any sense, the Afghan national army must be of sufficient size and skill to take over the security duties that the warlords' militias now provide to local populations. Creating a conventional army out of whole cloth is a difficult task at any time; doing so while the Taliban and al-Qaeda are attempting to regain power will make the process in Afghanistan even more challenging. Moreover, we are not sure that we *want* all of these groups disarmed as quickly as some wish. In the fight against the Taliban and other jihadists in southern and eastern Afghanistan, the militias are as invaluable today as they were in the 2001 campaign that drove out the Taliban and al-Qaeda. To disarm and disband them in the absence of a force that can take their place would be tantamount to granting Mullah Omar a foothold in the country.

The resurgence of the Taliban is what worries us most. In the fall of 2003, the Taliban began trying to make good on its public threat to take over the country by attacking NATO forces and killing aid workers. The Taliban and al-Qaeda also have taken their activities in the "tribal" territories of Pakistan, the areas along the Pakistan–Afghanistan border to include the cities of Peshawar and Quetta.

Pakistan must act—assisted by coalition forces on the Afghan side of the border—to eliminate this al-Qaeda and Taliban presence. Destroying the Taliban and al-Qaeda would remove the greatest threat not only to Afghanistan but to the Pakistani government as well. Pakistan's intelligence service helped create the Taliban and see it into power. Now the Taliban is a potential threat to the Pakistani government in a country where radical Islam has a deep reservoir of public support.

At present, the United States has approximately 11,000 troops in Afghanistan, and along with fighting the terrorists, our government is committed to a necessary program of domestic improvements throughout the country. Currently, Provincial Reconstruction Teams (PRTs) are developing the areas outside of Kabul. Led by Americans, Germans, and workers from other NATO countries, the PRTs are proving to be very effective at planning, developing, and executing the reconstruction projects aimed at improving infrastructure, establishing schools, and restoring legitimate agriculture to attract some farmers away from growing opium poppies. Their operations as well as those of various aid agencies must be expanded—and protected—throughout the country. The Afghans must come to believe that the government in Kabul and its international allies are offering Afghanistan a better future. The key to ensuring a stable, peaceful Afghanistan is to stay the course. Allowing Afghanistan's economic and political development to languish and its security system to deteriorate would be to recreate the conditions that led to the establishment of the Taliban regime. We will likely be in Afghanistan, assisting in its development, for another ten to twenty years. But to defeat terrorism, we have no choice.

The force level we need to maintain in Afghanistan is relatively small, the duties in the long term, relatively easy. The fact that we will be keeping troops in Afghanistan (and other countries) for decades is not to say that the Web of Terror can't be defeated quickly. We defeated the Axis powers within four years of our entry into World War II—and yet we still have troops in German and Japan, sixty years later. So too in the war against terror we must act with a swift sword, as we did in Afghanistan, while recognizing that a longer-term military presence in the country is a necessary burden, and not an intolerable one.

Iraq

We were not at all surprised—and, in fact, predicted—that the Iraqi military would collapse rapidly in the face of the American-led coalition. We also are not entirely surprised at the failure of inspectors to find the weapons of mass destruction that every intelligence agency in the world believed that Saddam Hussein had. We are not surprised because we believe we know where these weapons are: in Syria and Syrian-controlled areas of Lebanon. And we believe they will be found, if not by the United States then by Israel, which has an overwhelming interest in keeping these weapons out of the hands of terrorist groups—an interest that won't be swayed by diplomatic niceties.

What already has been found in Iraq is an astonishing amount of conventional weapons in stockpiles throughout the country. In one unit's area of operations in Iraq, there were sixty-two ammunition supply points, one of which had more than 4,000 rocket-propelled grenades, along with other weapons and ammunition, in its inventory. One Army explosive ordnance disposal expert predicted that, using normal procedures, it would take *seventeen years* to get rid of the conventional weapons amassed by Saddam Hussein.

Another big surprise in Iraq is how "rotten" Iraq was by the spring of 2003. We knew that Saddam Hussein's military had been downgraded by years of sanctions; that is why we were confident the bulk of the Iraqi army would not put up much of a fight. What was a surprise was how thoroughly those decades of corruption and ineptitude on the part of Saddam Hussein and his cronies, and the years of economic sanctions against Iraq had hollowed out the country's infrastructure. Although Iraq's public infrastructure was not a target for coalition airpower, when coalition forces liberated Iraq, they found that the country's public utilities essentially were lashed together by baling wire and chewing gum.

And of course, the economy of Iraq is a mess. It was dilapidated to begin with. But the disruption of war and the disbanding of the Iraqi army brought the combined rate of underemployment and unemployment, according to one intelligence officer, to at least 60 percent and perhaps as high as 80 percent.

As with Afghanistan, however, the most pressing concern in Iraq will be security. Iraq has become the front line for the jihadists in their war against the West and moderate Islam. And it will remain a combat zone until the jihadists find their situation untenable. Part of that battle will be fought by us, part by the de-Ba'athified Iraqi police and army, and part by our reconstruction efforts that need to have as their objective providing full employment for the Iraqi people.

While we expect American forces to be deployed in Iraq for the next two decades, it will be an ever-shrinking number of troops. Indeed, by the spring of 2004, our military presence in Iraq already had been reduced from seventeen brigades to fourteen brigades. These numbers will continue to fall until we have deployed as few as three or four brigades, with a strong contingent of U.S. aircraft deployed in air bases near Baghdad and in southern Iraq.

Some critics of U.S. policy chide the Bush administration for "going it alone" in Iraq, for being "unilateral." The solution for all of Iraq's problems, they assert, is to "internationalize" the security and reconstruction effort. The fact is the effort already is internationalized and was from the beginning. As of February 2004, there were approximately 28,000 troops—roughly the equivalent of two U.S. Army divisions or six U.S. Army brigades—drawn from more than thirty countries in Iraq. Beyond their numbers, the soldiers of the multinational force are professionals, proud of their work, and respected by our own troops. And they have staying power. For example, the Dutch contingent arrived in Iraq equipped with mortars, heavy machine guns, and armored vehicles—in other words, ready for a fight. This is a positive contrast to the 200 lightly armed Dutch peacekeepers under UN command who, in 1995, were unable to defend the Bosnian town of Srebrenica against a Serbian assault—and to prevent the resulting massacre of 7,500 Muslim men and boys.

After dozens of UN employees were killed in a truck bomb attack on the organization's headquarters in Baghdad in August 2003, the first reaction of the UN and other international aid organizations was to quit Iraq. Only now are they starting to talk about returning, and they have sent an exploratory team to Iraq to consider the future deployment of UN teams specifically to help with the Iraqi election process. In contrast, when the soldiers of our coalition partners Italy, Poland, and Spain were killed in Iraq, their respective governments did not retreat. It makes no sense to cede control of Iraq's security and reconstruction to the UN, an organization that already has a bad track record of doing nothing while people are massacred—as in the Balkans, among other hot spots—and that retreated in the face of violence in Iraq, rather than continue to trust the already deployed international force that has the courage necessary to win.

As of February 2004, there were up to 200,000 trained Iraqi security forces with a target number of 300,000, and probably more dependent upon the jihadist insurgency, by the end of 2004. These security forces are composed of the Army, Border Patrol, Police, Facility Protections Services, and Civil Defense forces. We agree that these numbers should be increased as scheduled to 300,000. This is a challenge, because many of these units will receive their final training "on the job," and because special care must be taken to ensure that Ba'athist diehards and radical Islamists do not infiltrate their ranks. Aggressive tactics—

hunting down diehard antigovernment fighters, uncovering their caches of money and weapons, and denying them other sources of support—are what will keep the Ba'athists and jihadists off-balance. Our own troops can be more aggressive militarily if Iraqi forces are doing the internal security and police work as well as developing intelligence sources—tasks for which the Iraqis are better suited than are we, knowing as they do the people and the culture in ways that we can never hope to rival.

The Iraqi army and newly formed Iraqi border police need to be large enough to shut down Iraq's borders to the Ba'athists, the jihadists, and those who supply them with manpower and money. On some of Iraq's borders, the number of jihadists slipping across is relatively small. Our sources tell us that along Iraq's long border with Saudi Arabia perhaps only two or three a night, sometimes as many as five, come across (although in one incident, seventy-five jihadists were intercepted and killed). Once across, however, they can be hard to trace, because their contacts provide them with forged Iraqi identity papers. Iraqi soldiers and police officers could identify them as foreigners by their accents and methods of speech, but coalition troops are unlikely to note the differences. Even if the number of incoming jihadists is only a trickle, it still amounts to 60 to 150 fighters a month coming in from across the Saudi border alone, and adding a hundred terrorists a month to the already volatile situation in Iraq can mean a lot of trouble. But it shouldn't—because we have the technology to track down those trying to get into Iraq. We could significantly improve the surveillance of the border areas with high-technology observation equipment. Deploying such technology as the Global Hawk, the latest word in long-endurance, high-flying unmanned aerial vehicles (UAVs), can help prevent troublemakers from Iran, Syria, and Saudi Arabia from getting into Iraq.

We must also make the most of our efforts to restore "normal life" in Iraq, creating the conditions in which children can walk safely to school, electricity is reliable, and fresh, drinkable water comes out of every opened tap. Although we are making unheralded strides and achieving everyday victories in the restoration of public education and public services, that is only part of the job. The physical infrastructure of Iraq must be restored so that commerce can thrive. The big victory, however, will come when a democratic civil life—what Americans would consider "normal"—takes root and blooms in Iraq. When the Iraqis gain a stake in their own government through an electoral process that is stable and repeatable (they must avoid the "One Man–One Vote–One Time" trap), and when responsibility for public services, such as water and schools, lies with local authorities, our job in the country will be done. Iraq then will be ready to care for itself.

Perhaps the most promising aspect of Iraqi civic renewal is the sudden appearance of more than 150 newspapers and magazines in the country since its liberation—though as we will discuss later, it is hugely important that the United States do a much better job of promoting the expansion of growth of news media that can broadcast democratic values. The media is wild and free in Iraq now, but that does not mean it cannot only deliver bazaar gossip and rumor and not help the Iraqis become a more informed citizenry.

The people of Iraq are about to be granted political decision-making power of a sort that no living Iraqi has ever known, and we do not underestimate the difficulties of building a lasting democracy and durable economy in Iraq. Iraq needs our support to guarantee the three S's: security, services, and salaries. As you might expect, these are interrelated tasks. Our military forces—with their presence, firepower, operations, and, most especially, training of Iraqi forces—can buttress the Iraqis' efforts to secure their country's infrastructure against acts of sabotage and other disruptions. As soon as the efficient delivery services—water, electricity, transportation, broadcasting—become commonplace through the work of the foreign corporations that are rebuilding and improving Iraq's infrastructure with job creation, there will be fewer grounds for political disaffection and greater cause for economic confidence. Given the county's large oil deposits, as soon as the oil production system has been restored and can be protected against sabotage, wealth will flow into the government's coffers that can be used to make even more improvements in Iraq's public services, which in turn will spur even more economic activity, especially by the Iraqi businesses, large and small, that are springing up all over that country. In short, a sound Iraqi economy and thus a stable Iraqi social and civic life are very achievable goals.

There is a lot the United States and other nations can do to deliver jobs, an infrastructure that works, and public safety, and so strengthen the prospects for the rise of a stable, democratic Iraq. Just as important, however, there is one thing we *cannot* do: withdraw precipitately from Iraq. Having been on the scene, we know what it will take—and we know how much our work is valued. In September 2003, we traveled to the Persian Gulf for a weeklong Defense Department–sponsored trip. We spent much of the time in Iraq. Everywhere—*everywhere*—we went we encountered Iraqis who told us quite plainly how happy they were that the United States had overthrown Saddam Hussein. Yes, they were not happy about the lack of public services and the dearth of jobs, but they welcomed the opportunity to develop a democratic civil society. Repeatedly, the conversations would end with the Iraqi to whom we were speaking saying, "Thank you, America, for liberating us." We know from reading the polls, and from firsthand experience, that the Iraqi people want us to stay; and stay we should until the situation is secure. It is imperative that we accelerate the reconstruction dollars into the country. Unfortunately, we are using peacetime rules for the contractor evaluations in a wartime situation. This is causing undue delay and should be rectified immediately.

On a broader strategic scale, a rapid withdrawal of American forces before Iraq is secure and stable would only underline our enemies' canard that the United States does not have the stomach for anything resembling a protracted struggle and undermine our credibility as an ally to those regimes in the region and around the world that might seek our assistance to repel radical Islamists' attempts to overthrown them.

Iran

In many aspects, Iran seems a more formidable enemy than Iraq. It has a larger population, a more challenging terrain, and a military not degraded by years of sanctions. That said, Iran is very likely to fall more easily than Iraq did, because Iran's domestic opposition is developing into a serious threat to the regime.

Iran reminds us of the Soviet Union circa 1989. It is a large country with a huge population (more than sixty-eight million), and it should be a rich country, sitting as it does on huge reserves of oil. The country's wealth, however, does not make it down to the majority of Iranians. Instead, approximately 40 percent of Iranians live in poverty, because the clerics who control Iranian political and economic life siphon off much of the national income for their own uses.

The Constitution of the Soviet Union promised numerous rights to its citizens. Likewise, the Iranian constitution presents a façade of political freedom. It has an elected parliament and a democratically elected president. The catch, however, is that the constitution also vests all ultimate power in an nonelected body of six clerics and six religious lawyers, the Guardian Council, and the post of Supreme Ruler, a cleric chosen by another nonelected body, the House of Experts.

For many years, the Islamic Republic apparently was popular within Iran. However, over time, many Iranians have come to oppose the theocratic nature of the Iranian state and resent the concentration of political and economic power in the hands of the mullahs, their families, and their cronies. Among the youth of Iran there are many who find Western political forms and even elements of Western culture more attractive than the political and cultural construct offered by the mullahs. In fact, judging from recent political developments in

Iran, it appears that the rule of the mullahs survives only because they manipulate Iran's political process. Democratic reform won't happen naturally in Iran—because the mullahs probably will block it, using their constitutional power and, if that fails to stem the tide of democratization, the quasi-official paramilitary forces at their command, their own versions of the militias and "fedayeen" of Ba'athist Iraq. It cannot be denied, however, that the people of Iran are ready and eager for it. The broadly popular Iranian movement in favor of democracy deserves our support for three simple reasons: the Iranian people want to be free, they deserve to be free, and the Web of Terror will greatly diminish when they are free.

For these reasons, the United States and other free nations should offer the democratic opposition everything we can to help them spread their message: satellite phones, computers, fax machines, even satellite radio and television stations, Voice of America broadcasts, and so on. Our goal should be to help the democratic opposition achieve the same impact on Iran that Solidarity had in Communist Poland. Our president should make it clear that our country stands behind the ambitions of the Iranian people for freedom. And if we succeed in creating a stable, democratic Iraq, the president's words will have a very tangible meaning for the people in Iran.

As encouraging as the growing strength of the pro-democracy movement in Iran is, we cannot wait for moral suasion and quiet diplomacy to have some effect on the mullahs. They are a key strand in the Web of Terror, and their nuclear ambitions are dangerously close to fulfillment.

The Iranians insist that their nuclear program is devoted to civilian purposes, to provide electricity. In September 2003, however, inspectors of the UN's International Atomic Energy Agency reported that they had discovered highly enriched (weapons-grade) uranium on equipment at an Iranian nuclear site. This discovery—and other reports concerning the Iranian nuclear program, including some that we heard directly from Israeli and Indian diplomats—brings into question the CIA's oft-cited analysis that Iran would have nuclear weapons in two to three *years*. We remember all too well the shock that occurred when, after the 1991 Persian Gulf War, international inspectors discovered that Saddam Hussein's nuclear program was much farther along than prewar intelligence estimates had claimed. We also now know—thanks to Libya's about-face on its WMD programs—that Libya was much farther along in developing nuclear weapons than anyone imagined. There is no reason to be sanguine and there is every reason to be worried about how far Iran has gone and is going in its nuclear program.

If Iran develops nuclear weapons, so might other countries in the region. Saudi Arabia, for instance, already has as many as fifty Chinese-made intermediate-range ballistic missiles. Saudi Arabian officials have met with Pakistan's President Musharraf, and, as we recently discovered, Pakistan has a history of selling nuclear technology and nuclear know-how, including apparently to Iran, North Korea, and Libya. We have no way of knowing what the Pakistani nuclear establishment might have sold to Riyadh in the way of equipment, advice, and documents related to nuclear weapons or the Pakistani army might have exchanged as a quid pro quo for Saudi financial support of the Taliban and Pakistan-sponsored Islamist rebels in Kashmir. It is imperative that Pakistan disclose all of its nuclear proliferation dealings with other countries.

More important is the question of Israel's reaction to Iran's nuclear weapons program. On January 4, 2004, the Israeli Defense Minister, Shaul Mofaz, an Iranian-born Israeli, spoke to the Iranian people via a radio broadcast. Speaking in his native Farsi, General Mofaz bluntly told his listeners that Israel would not accept an Iranian nuclear bomb. Only a couple of weeks later, we met with Israeli diplomats who underlined Mofaz's comments. They also confirmed information we received in 2003: Israel considers a preemptive strike against Iran's nuclear facilities as a serious possibility. There is precedent for such a strike. In 1981, in a brilliantly planned and executed attack, the

Israeli Air Force destroyed Iraq's French-built Osirak nuclear reactor, an act that was publicly condemned and privately welcomed in the region and around the world.

In Rowan Scarborough's book, *Rumsfeld's War*, it was revealed that the Israeli defense forces have eighty-two nuclear weapons as part of their nuclear deterrence force. In our research for this book, we discovered that a group of countries, led by Israel and the U.S., had been working since 1981 on a mega-secret project to develop and deploy a weapon system that can neutralize nuclear weapons. The highly advanced, space-deployable, BHB weapon system, code-named XXXBHB-BACAR-1318-I390MSCH, has extraordinary potential and is a key part of the West's deterrence strategy. For the past twenty-five years, the project and the scientists involved in it were kept in strict secrecy and their existence denied. The scientists rejected Nobel Physics prize and Nobel Peace prize nominations and have been repeatedly and deliberately the subject of intense military disinformation through the media in order to divert attention from their highly secretive work. In 1981, when CIA director William J. Casey signed onto the SDI (Strategic Defense Initiative)—a missile defense shield against incoming nuclear warheads—he gave the green light for the technology's development for deterrence purposes and peaceful use only. Although we have only limited information, it appears that Iran's rapidly developing nuclear capabilities could be neutralized and rendered obsolete, as could the capabilities of other rogue countries.

Moreover, Iran continues to be a major state sponsor of terrorism with such clients as Hezbollah, Palestinian Islamic Jihad, and Yasser Arafat's Palestinian Authority. Iranian support of these groups is coordinated by agents of Iran's Ministry of Intelligence and Security (MOIS) and the Iranian Revolutionary Guard Corps (also known as the Pasdaran), organizations that have been used by the mullahs to export Iranian-style Islamic revolution throughout the region for decades. In early January 2004, an American intelligence officer confirmed to us that there are also al-Qaeda operatives in Iran—and Iran has refused to turn over these terrorists to the United States.

A pro-Western, democratic regime in Iraq is, obviously, a threat to the Iranian mullahs' legitimacy because it would provide a rallying point for Iranian exiles and would-be democratic reformers. If the mullahs continue to run Iran, they will try to destroy a democratic Iraq. It was not a surprise, therefore, when we learned from a CIA officer that the MOIS already is active in the Shi'ite areas of Iraq, often in support of extremist Shi'ite clerics. We cannot tolerate Iranian support for terrorism, including attempts to subvert Iraq. But most of all, we cannot tolerate Iran's development of nuclear weapons.

The president must first inform Iran in the bluntest language possible that developing nuclear weapons is a red line it cannot cross. The president should not only immediately invoke his statutory authority to impose sanctions against corporations that do business with Iran's oil industry, but also encourage foreign governments to do the same. Japan needs to be encouraged to crack down on its corporations by a direct appeal to its self-interest: Every Japanese corporation that invests in Iran's oil industry is making a de facto investment in Iran's nuclear weapons cooperation with North Korea—and North Korea has Japan as a target. Likewise, the United States must urge Russia and Germany to pull their support from Iran's civilian nuclear program; the technology and know-how is too easily transferred to weapons programs. It might be worth approaching France with a request to restrict its support of Iran's nuclear program if only to give the world another example of the French government's boundless venality.

The United States must prepare to approach the UN Security Council with a draft resolution for a total economic embargo on Iran, the seizing of Iranian assets (to be held in trust for future Iranian government), and a strict naval quarantine in the Persian Gulf and the Strait of Hormuz. The United Nations would lift the embargo only when the Iran government dismantles its nuclear weapons program under the supervision of international inspections. Libya (and before Libya, South Africa) has given Iran an example to follow on how to dismantle a nuclear weapons program in a way that meets international standards of verification. Iran would be required to surrender or destroy all equipment needed to produce fissionable materials (highly enriched uranium and plutonium), all long-range ballistic missiles, and all cruise missiles; release all documents related to its nuclear weapons program; and expel all foreign scientists, technicians, and engineers involved in nuclear weapons design, development, and production. Because the French or Russians are likely to veto—or, at least, threaten to veto—such a Security Council resolution, the United States should be ready to impose these conditions on Iran with a coalition of our own. If that coalition is, in the end, composed solely of the United States, the Gulf States, Great Britain, Australia, Japan, and India, it would be enough.

A strict "no sanctuary" policy regarding terrorists is an essential part of the global strategy against terrorism. Therefore, the United States should be prepared to give Iran another dose of strong antiterror medicine by using airpower to strike terrorist sanctuaries within Iran. If Iran allows al-Qaeda or other jihadist groups to set up shop or take refuge within its borders, it must pay the price of being an accessory to and abettor of terrorism.

The Iranian mullahs' support for terrorism, their repression of their own people who so obviously yearn to be free, and their appalling human rights record are reasons enough to change the regime. Their ambitious nuclear weapons program makes regime change in Iran more than desirable; it makes it necessary—now. And to achieve that, we should deploy every lever we have—diplomatic, economic, and even military—until we get the necessary result.

North Korea

North Korea created its nuclear weapons program for money, which means, *for export.* North Korean scientists, engineers, and technicians are in Tehran and other cities in Iran, working for Iran's nuclear weapons program. North Korea is developing and selling ballistic missiles to Iran, Syria, and Yemen (and probably to other customers that we might not know about now). Pakistan has admitted that it traded its expertise related to nuclear weapons to North Korea for North Korea's expertise in ballistic missile technology.

In an August 5, 2003, op-ed in the *Wall Street Journal,* Jim Woolsey, former director of the CIA, and Tom wrote a lengthy article on resolving the problems with North Korea. In it they describe how the North Koreans use their nuclear weapons program *for extortion.* Not only has North Korea violated agreements not to pursue nuclear weapons and withdrawn from the Nuclear Non-Proliferation Treaty, it has demanded what is essentially a bribe to turn the program off again. North Korea expects that if it rattles its nuclear weapons and ballistic missiles enough, it will succeed, as it has in the past, in shaking money and material aid from the United States and Japan. Its transparently mercenary motives, however, shouldn't disguise the fact that the North Korean nuclear threat is very real.

In early July 2003, krypton 85—a gas produced when spent nuclear fuel is reprocessed into plutonium for nuclear weapons—was detected in an area removed from North Korea's only known reprocessing facility at Yongbyon. In January 2004, North Korea showed an unofficial delegation of American nuclear experts who were touring its nuclear facilities that it removed spent fuel rods from the holding ponds where earlier nuclear inspectors had put them and sent them away for "reprocessing." When North Korea ousted international inspectors and left the Nuclear Non-Proliferation Treaty in January 2002, it had 8,000 spent fuel rods at the Yongbyon facility. If they indeed have been reprocessed, North Korea's dictator Kim Jong Il might have material for several nuclear weapons (he is already suspected of having one or two).

The news gets worse. In the fall of 2003, the CIA declared that North Korea's nuclear weapons program is sufficiently sophisticated that it will not have to explode a nuclear bomb in order to determine if its weapons will work. That means that the world might not know North Korea has operational weapons until it actually uses one, or another rogue state or a terrorist group detonates one of the weapons North Korea has sold it in Los Angeles, Tel Aviv, New Delhi, or London. Given North Korea's boast in April 2003 that it would sell weapons-grade plutonium to whomever it pleased, there is no gainsaying the fact that the North Korean nuclear threat is enormous and pressing.

There is no realistic way to stop North Korea from exporting plutonium—and even manufactured weapons—to potential customers, which would include rogue states and terrorist organizations. North Korea already clandestinely ships ballistic missiles to customers all over the world. Former Secretary of Defense William Perry observed that the amount of plutonium needed for a bomb is about the size of a soccer ball. It would be easy for the North Koreans to use air shipments, including those protected by diplomatic immunity, to smuggle nuclear materials and/or bomb components to their customers.

So how do we stop North Korea? There are two options. First, North Korea is dependent on China for food, fuel, and financial support. China needs to understand that if North Korea goes ahead with its nuclear weapons program, then Japan, Taiwan, and even South Korea could follow—and Northeast Asia would be "nuclearized." The president of the United States should remind the Chinese that this scenario is not in their interest, and remind them too that he and South Korea's president, Roh Moo-hyun, signed a joint declaration in May 2003 that they will "not tolerate nuclear weapons in North Korea."

The Chinese might eschew such a forceful course of action—as they have in the past. North Korea is their ally after all. Or China might demand concessions related to Taiwan that the United States would find intolerable. That means the United States needs to develop other options. Many U.S. policymakers reflexively reject the use of force against North Korea, casting any conflict on the Korean peninsula in nightmarish terms. The Chinese and North Koreans know this, and take advantage of it. To put it bluntly, they do not expect American action. To restore our diplomatic credibility and to have an effective response if war becomes unavoidable, however, the United States and South Korea must come together—initially in secret, if necessary—and begin to assess realistically what it would take to change the North Korean regime by military means.

A surgical strike against the nuclear site at Yongbyon would be insufficient, not only because there might be other nuclear sites, but because we must protect South Korea from attack, particularly from the masses of North Korean artillery just north of the Demilitarized Zone. We must prepare to win a war, not merely execute a strike.

To our advantage, the U.S. and South Korean militaries have spent more than fifty years preparing to fight and win a war against North Korea. Massive airpower is the key to being able both to destroy Yongbyon and to protect South Korea from attack by missiles or artillery. There are many hardened air bases available in South Korea, and the South Koreans have an excellent air force of approximately 550 modern tactical aircraft.

The United States should begin planning to deploy the Patriot tactical ballistic missile defense system in South Korea. We should also deploy U.S. Navy warships equipped with the Aegis system to shoot down ballistic missiles fired at South Korea and Japan. The United States also should reinforce its tactical air forces in the area, moving several air wings to Japan and South Korea, putting aircraft carrier battle groups in the Western Pacific, and deploying surveillance aircraft and drones.

All these elements must be movable on short notice in order that, once "the balloon goes up" in Korea, that U.S. and South Korean air forces can launch well over 4,000 sorties a day (compared with 800 in Iraq). Considering that the vast majority of these sorties would use precision munitions, and that surveillance aircraft would permit immediate targeting of artillery pieces and ballistic missile launch sites, the use of air power in such a war would be swifter and more devastating than it was in Iraq.

North Korea's obsolescent air defenses—both fighter aircraft and ground-based missiles—would not last long. Most of North Korea's armed forces are along the DMZ. Smash them in a ferocious air campaign and the rest of the country is open to ground operations by U.S. and South Korean forces. Marine forces deployed off both coasts of North Korea could put both Pyongyang and Wonsan at risk of rapid seizure, particularly given the fact that most of North Korea's armed forces are situated along the DMZ.

In addition, the South Korean army is well equipped and well trained. With help from perhaps two additional U.S. Army divisions, it could drive quickly and deeply into North Korea. In fact, our combined forces could defeat North Korea decisively in thirty to sixty days. There is no doubt on the outcome. If North Korea refuses to end its nuclear program—and if China refuses to force North Korea to end it—we need to make it clear that we will act decisively to take out North Korea's weapons and its noxious regime. We can and we must.

Syria

Syria is a domino waiting to fall. It is an enormous supporter of terrorism—but it lacks the oil wealth of Iran, Saudi Arabia, Libya, and Iraq. It is a ruthless police state—but its base of support is Alawite Muslims, who make up about 11 percent of the population. It is the last Ba'ath Party–controlled state; its deep-pocketed Ba'athist neighbor, Saddam Hussein, is gone.

And most important for us are reports that Saddam Hussein sent chemical, biological, and other weapons or weapons components to three locations in Syria. The first is in northern Syria in a tunnel complex used by the Syrians for their own WMD called al Baida. The second location is a Syrian Air Force Camp near Tai Snan. The third location is in southern Syria, near the Lebanese border, in a city called Sjinsjam, itself close to the city of Homs. Weapons also could be hid-

den in sites in the Bekaa Valley. Saddam Hussein and his henchmen
sent these weapons as well as hundreds of millions of dollars in cash
to Syria for "safekeeping." With Saddam Hussein's regime gone, however, cash-strapped Syria will keep the cash and sell these weapons to
the several terrorist groups that look to Syria for support, among them
Hezbollah and Hamas. Israel would be the target. Israel knows the
weapons are present in Syria, and, therefore, we would not be surprised to see preemptive Israeli strikes against Syria to prevent these
weapons from being transferred to these terrorist groups.

It is hardly surprising that Syria made diplomatic overtures to the
United States after Operation Iraqi Freedom. It is in a difficult geo-
strategic position, ringed by Israel, Turkey, and American forces in Iraq.
Syria's economy is weak and its major source of revenue—helping Saddam Hussein beat the oil embargo on Iraq—now is gone. The Syrian
regime has little popular support—and its leaders know it. While
impressive to some on paper, Syria's military is unimpressive in reality. In short, Syria cannot bargain from a position of strength and, therefore, it would be unconscionable for the United States to delay acting
quickly and decisively to cut Syria out of the Web of Terror.

For their part, the Syrians hope to give the United States just
enough cooperation to prevent military action, and perhaps even gain
economic aid, while continuing to serve as the conduit of Iran's support to Palestinian terror groups and aiding the broader Web of Terror.
The United States must end Syria's double game immediately by issu-
ing an ultimatum to Syria's president, Bashar Assad: expel all terror
groups from Syrian soil and Syrian-controlled Lebanon, give up all
Iraqi weapons of mass destruction, and stop letting Iranian cadres,
weapons, and money pass through your country to Palestinian terror
groups—or the United States and a coalition of the willing will topple
your regime.

Facing the Mediterranean Sea, Syria is an ideal place to use America's dominant sea and air power. Coalition forces would move
quickly into Syria and the Bekaa Valley, guiding precision air strikes

on terrorist training camps, harassing any terrorists who flee U.S. air assaults, and seeking storage sites for weapons of mass destruction. Delivering reinforcements quickly at key points would be a relatively simple affair.

Bashar Assad should be made to realize that he has two options: cooperate with the civilized world against terror, as Colonel Gaddafi is apparently doing, or be toppled like Saddam Hussein.

Saudi Arabia

The House of Saud is now locked in a fight for its life against Islamist terror.

On May 12, 2003, al-Qaeda struck in Riyadh, killing twelve people in suicide car bomb attacks. In the fall of 2003, terrorists struck again in Riyadh, attacking a compound in which foreign workers, many of them Lebanese Christians, were killed and wounded. Another worrisome aspect of this attack was that some of the attackers wore Saudi Arabian police uniforms and drove Saudi Arabian police cars.

To his credit, the de facto leader of Saudi Arabia, Crown Prince Abdullah, responded forcibly. Saudi security forces have killed dozens of al-Qaeda terrorists, many in ferocious gun battles, and arrested hundreds of suspected al-Qaeda operatives and their supporters. The Saudi authorities also have uncovered large caches of arms as well as bundles of documents related to al-Qaeda's financial records.

Al-Qaeda has many fighters and supporters within Saudi Arabia. As one analyst told us, only about 25 percent of the Saudi population wholeheartedly supports the royal family. Ironically, the inflexible Wahhabis Islam preached by Saudi-funded clerics in mosques, taught in Saudi-funded schools, and put into action by Saudi-supported Islamist groups around the world is what inspires the anti-monarchist forces. The chickens have come home to roost for the House of Saud. It now is fighting the very terrorism that it helped create.

That might seem poetic justice to some, but the United States has an interest in Saudi reform rather than revolution. In the late 1970s, the United States stood by while the Shah of Iran fell and an Islamic republic took his place. That foreign policy mistake gave rise to the mullahs and eventually the Web of Terror that constitutes the greatest post-Communist threat to the Western world. The United States, therefore, cannot make the same mistake in Saudi Arabia that it did in Iran. We cannot let anti-American mullahs replace another monarchy in the Persian Gulf region.

The House of Saud is a seething mess of competing factions—and, therefore, the Kingdom's government often seems to be of two minds (at least), with some of its members assuring the West that it stands with it against terrorism as others pursue those policies that help spread the stern Wahhabi Islam that often drives Islamist terror. The infuriating fact remains, however, that, in the short term at least, the United States must support the House of Saud. We must continue to provide material assistance and training to the Saudi military and the kingdom's security forces in their now almost daily battles with Islamist terrorists.

That said, it is time for the United States to put the House of Saud on notice. Business as usual isn't good enough. The Kingdom's recent tough response to domestic terrorism—striking with "an iron fist," as the Crown Prince colorfully puts it—is an admirable one; as the Shah discovered in 1979, however, that can only go so far in preserving a dynasty. The Kingdom needs to reform its economy, domestic politics, and foreign policy immediately.

The president should be clear: Saudi Arabia must close "the Islamic interests" section in every Saudi Arabian embassy and stop its support and promotion of Islamic schools and mosques that promote Wahhabi Islam, Islamic "charities," and other incubators of terror. For too long, the House of Saud has assumed that by funding radical Islam it could tame and divert it. In fact, the Saudis have a created a monster that threatens the Islamic world and the West and now the monarchy itself. The Kingdom of Saudi Arabia spends hundreds of millions of dollars a year supporting radical Wahhabi Islam around the world, funding terrorist groups like Palestinian Islamic Jihad and Hamas, and making payments to the families of Palestinian suicide bombers. This money should be better spent reforming the Saudi education system so that it teaches job skills, not hatred of "infidels." Saudi Arabia's neighbor, Qatar, provides a perfect model for reform of the Saudi education system. In 2003, under the sponsorship of the Emir of Qatar and his wife, Qatar established "Education City," a 2,400-acre facility in cooperation with such institutions as Texas A&M, Cornell University Medical School, and the Rand Corporation. Not only do the institutions of "Education City" offer schooling, they spur research and development that can improve the quality of life for the people. Soon, the Qatar government will begin a reform of its elementary and secondary education system. One of its specific goals is to develop an appreciation of other cultures and religions, to foster tolerance and understanding, rather than hatred and terrorism. If Saudi Arabia—with its much greater wealth—followed Qatar's lead, it could become *the* major center of learning *in all disciplines* (not just in Wahhabi theology), in the Arab world, indeed in the Islamic world.

As the Shah of Iran discovered in the late 1970s, however, establishing a quality education system is not enough. There must be jobs for the well-educated graduates. And that means reforming Saudi Arabia's economy so that it is no longer almost solely dependent on the extraction of mineral wealth, but is a diversified market economy from which Saudi Arabia can derive widespread economic prosperity as other Gulf States—like Qatar, Bahrain, Dubai, and Abu Dhabi—have done. Taking a cue from other Muslim monarchies, such as Morocco, Qatar, and Bahrain, the leadership of Saudi Arabia should begin the process of transforming the kingdom's political system from a family business into a constitutional monarchy, complete with a written constitution and a sound and open legal system in which any citizen can expect justice. If the House of Saud persists in treating Saudi Arabia as a family possession run solely for the family's benefit, the dynasty's future will be imperiled, no matter how successful its current crackdown against internal terrorism.

If the House of Saud does not follow an American diplomatic lead to reform along the lines we've sketched, it could easily fall to an Islamist revolution. So the United States must dust off the contingency plans to meet that threat, which would mean invading Saudi Arabia, seizing its oil fields, production facilities, and tanker terminals, securing and isolating them from the Islamists—and defeating them with the assistance of the more Western-oriented princes, who need to be identified now, who can lead a counterrevolutionary opposition. Other Gulf States, like Qatar and Kuwait, would certainly come to our aid.

On the subject of Saudi Arabia, two words are enough to prevent some U.S. policymakers from acting aggressively to save the regime: *Mecca* and *Medina*, the two holiest cities in Islam. The presence of American forces in Saudi Arabia inflamed Osama bin Laden and prompted the Khobar Towers bombing. But a radical Islamic takeover would be worse than any reaction to American troops in Saudi Arabia. With the help of the other Gulf States and with reformist pro-Western Saudi princes, we can turn back that terrorist threat.

Pakistan

Pakistan is balancing on a razor's edge. The two assassination attempts against President Pervez Musharraf in December 2003 show how tenuous the situation is in Pakistan. Like Saudi Arabia, Pakistan is divided between a pro-Western faction and a large and powerful Islamist faction. Pakistan considers itself a leading Islamic country. Its constitution enshrines sharia law. It has the only Islamic nuclear weapon—so far. And, unfortunately, many within Pakistan, including some in its army and military intelligence service, supported the Taliban, which is now regrouping in the tribal areas of Pakistan along the Afghan border. Al-Qaeda's presence is reportedly growing. The country's religious schools continue to indoctrinate masses of students in the doctrines of radical Islam. And Pakistani nuclear scientists have made the rounds of rogue states, selling equipment and technical expertise to advance their nuclear weapons programs. Pakistan's future depends on its willingness to confront the Taliban, al-Qaeda, and other Islamist terrorist and terror-supporting groups within its own borders.

President Bush must press President Musharraf to continue investigating—and to halt—the "private" activities of Pakistani nuclear scientists, which it appears he has done with the admission of guilt by A. Q. Khan. Such activities have resulted in nuclear weapons knowledge going to Iran and North Korea. The United States needs to know the full extent and details of these breaches of security, so that we can have a better idea of how far developed are the nuclear weapons programs of these rogue states.

Like its nuclear-armed neighbor India, Pakistan is not a signatory to the Nuclear Non-Proliferation Treaty and, unless and until India unilaterally rids itself of its nuclear weapons, Pakistan is unlikely to become one. An Indo-Pakistani mutual nuclear disarmament treaty would be another diplomatic option—and a nation that India and Pakistan might consider an honest broker should be encouraged to propose the idea to them. India's long-term possession of nuclear weapons and its well-founded self-image as a country that is growing in international importance, however, probably would make that effort more than a little difficult.

In the probable absence of an Indo-Pakistani nuclear disarmament treaty, the United States and the United Kingdom could offer Pakistan an agreement in which Pakistan would strictly and effectively prohibit its nuclear establishment from engaging in any activities that would advance nuclear proliferation and, in exchange, the United States and the United Kingdom would provide increased economic and military aid to Pakistan.

Another important step for President Musharraf is to purge the Pakistani military—especially the army—of Islamist influences *before* he relinquishes his post as chief of staff of the Pakistani Army, a position he agreed to surrender by December 2004 in order to give Pakistan a

civilian-run government. The Pakistani army is the only national institution that has both the brains *and* the brawn to control Pakistan.
Turkey's military is the guarantor of a secular, democratic Turkey.
Musharraf needs to follow the Turkish model and make the Pakistani
army a bulwark against the radical Islamists. Moreover, he needs to
reorganize Pakistan's Inter-Service Intelligence (ISI), the military intelligence service that is best known for organizing, training, and arming
the mujahideen in Afghanistan during the 1980s. Unfortunately, it
also has been linked to terrorism in Indian-held Kashmir and is cred-
ited with being the organizing force behind the Taliban. The ISI has
outlived its usefulness to Pakistan, and if allowed to exist in its present form, has the potential to destabilize Pakistan as well as other
countries in South and Central Asia.

Related to reorganizing the ISI, Pakistan must eliminate the remnants of al-Qaeda and the Taliban from within its own borders. If President Musharraf asks for assistance in this effort, we must be willing
to provide everything from intelligence to air strikes, from transportation to conventional ground forces. It is risky for Musharraf to
act, but our diplomats need to point out that it is riskier for him not to
act—and that we will support him. Finally, we have to think of how
we would deal with the consequences of the unthinkable: the overthrow or assassination of President Musharraf and perhaps a conse-
quent civil war with the ultimate prize being nuclear weapons,
ballistic missiles, and the infrastructure to build more of them. America should work closely to safeguard Pakistan's nuclear arsenal and
keep nuclear warheads from falling under control of rogue commanders or Islamic terrorists. We should be prepared to give them U.S.
technology that will prevent Pakistan from launching its nuclear
weapons by rogue elements.

Israel-Palestine

Within the foreign policy establishment, it is an article of faith that settlement of the Israeli-Palestinian question is the key to peace in the

Middle East. Give the Palestinians a homeland of their own and suddenly peace will descend on the Middle East; radical Islam will lose
its appeal; and the lion will lie down with the lamb. All this is a
dream: a self-defeating, nonsensical dream.

Unfortunately, this dream has enormous power. It is the conventional wisdom—and a convenient excuse—in many capitals around
the world. In early January 2001, during the waning days of the Clinton administration, Yasser Arafat rejected what history probably will
record as the best deal for Palestinian statehood ever offered. The
Americans created—and Israel approved—a plan that would have
created a Palestinian state that covered more than 95 percent of the
West Bank and the Gaza Strip and would have allowed for Palestinian control of many of the religious sites in Jerusalem. If he had
accepted it, Yasser Arafat could have become a bona fide head of
state. Palestine could have become a magnet for returning immigrants, who would have used their expertise to create a vibrant business sector that would have provided jobs and economic growth.
Arafat, however, remained true to his blood-soaked revolutionary
roots and his directions from Tehran, Damascus, and Riyadh, and
took the Palestinians to war.

In this new intifada, the situation in Israel and Palestine has spi-
raled ever downward. Rather than take on the Israeli Defense Force in
a stand-up fight they would certainly lose, the Palestinian Authority
and its allies Hamas and Palestinian Islamic Jihad have embarked on
a terrorist campaign of suicide bombings, ambushes, and sniper
attacks. Sustained by weapons and explosives smuggled to the West
Bank and Gaza via tunnels that run to and from Egypt as well as
through southern Lebanon and Syria, this campaign has been all too
successful; the attacks have killed approximately one thousand
Israelis and injured another six thousand.

In retaliation, Israel has hunted down and killed many members of
the Palestinian terrorist organizations as well as reduced many of the
physical trappings of the Palestinian Authority to rubble. Instead of

living in his luxurious seaside villa and receiving fellow heads of state there, Arafat now hunkers down in the remnants of his West Bank compound in Ramallah, itself shattered in a 2002 siege. The tourist trade has evaporated, accelerating the decline of the Palestinian economy, now in shambles. Yet, because of the restraint—urged by the United States—that Israel has shown, and the financial support *still* provided to the Palestinian Authority by outside governments, many of the institutions of the Palestinian Authority remain up and running, and Palestinian and Arab television and radio continue to spew toxic anti-Israeli propaganda and encourage suicide bombings.

Even if he wanted to negotiate a lasting settlement with Israel—and that is extremely unlikely—Arafat is aging, his health is declining, and his life and liberty are dependent on Israeli sufferance. He is losing the authority he once had as *the* leader of the Palestinians. Despite his continuing efforts to "Islamify" himself and the Palestinian Authority, younger Palestinians shun Arafat. They flock instead to the banner of radical Islamist groups like Hamas and Palestinian Islamic Jihad and are influenced by the examples of the terrorists of Hezbollah. They have no interest in negotiating with Israel, only in destroying it.

Given these trends, Israel's decision to construct a security fence (the Seam Line) seems a prudent one—and not deserving of the criticism that many people, including some in the U.S. government, are directing at it. The wall will not only keep terrorists out, it will spare Israel—and the Palestinians—the otherwise inevitable Israeli counteroffensive against an ever more violent and ever more radicalized intifada. This security fence is already proving effective in preventing suicide bombers from entering into Israel from the West Bank.

The Israelis already understand what the rest of the world needs to understand: that a negotiated settlement with Yasser Arafat is a pipe dream. They also know that terror will not end with the creation of a Palestinian state, unless that Palestinian state is purged of terrorists. A Palestinian state allied to Iran, or a puppet of Syria, or full of terrorist groups like Palestinian Islamic Jihad and Hamas will not be "a partner for peace" but an implacable enemy. Only when the terrorists are beaten will a peaceful Palestinian state emerge.

For that to occur, the Palestinians themselves need to be lifted out from under the thumb of the terrorists and the kleptomaniacal Palestinian Authority. They both need and deserve what the people of Iraq now have: *liberation*. Liberation will begin when the Palestinian terror complex is cut off from its outside support—Syria, Iran, and Saudi Arabia are the chief culprits—and the terrorists are then given a choice: total war, which they will lose, or real peace. Put another way, the current policy relies on an *inside out* solution; our solution is to approach the problem from the *outside in.* The dictatorships of Syria and Iran should be toppled and the Kingdom of Saudi Arabia should be reformed, as we've outlined.

The liberation and transformation of Palestine represents a huge gamble. It means gambling that a Palestine purged of terrorists is a Palestine that will pursue peace with Israel and economic freedom for its own people. It is a gamble worth taking. Today, the Palestinians and the Israelis are living in intolerable conditions. The Palestinians are governed by an oppressive dictatorship that practices "crony capitalism" and political terror. The Israelis are forced to live lives in constant fear. To allow this situation to continue, to allow it to continue to serve as a rallying point for radical Islamic terror, is tantamount to criminal neglect. The risk is worth the likely gain.

THE GLOBAL WAR

We know the country-by-country strategy that we have outlined to end the Web of Terror might sound daunting, but it can be done. And it must be done. Al-Qaeda has a global presence. It is active in the Middle East and North Africa. It is increasingly active in Central Asia and Eastern Europe. It has cells in the West. It is active in Southeast Asia, Indonesia, and the Philippines. And it is in East Africa. America is fighting al-Qaeda, globally, and we are winning. But victory requires more than killing al-Qaeda's terrorists and freezing their accounts.

When World War II began for the United States after Pearl Harbor, our nation understood it had to defeat a great threat to world peace. Today we face another such threat, after the Pearl Harbor of September 11, 2001. We will achieve victory again. With the tools our nation has now, we can do it and, in relative terms, more easily than we did almost sixty years ago. And the stakes are just as high.

We can act now and win, or we can wait and let the danger grow— grow into the nightmare scenarios we sketched earlier. Any commander in chief who chooses the latter course has violated his obligation to defend the people of the United States. President Clinton's refusal to act in a decisive way against the murderous attacks by al-Qaeda against Americans overseas emboldened the terrorist to launch the September 11 attacks. No American president should make that mistake again. Declared enemies of the United States must be taken at their word. If not cooperative and they remain defiant, our message in response to them should be manifest: We will not tolerate your support of terrorism, and your regime will be changed unless you cooperate.

CHAPTER FOUR

INTO BATTLE: OPERATION ENDURING FREEDOM

I N LATE JANUARY 2004, President Hamid Karzai of Afghanistan signed the new constitution for Afghanistan. The document creates a democratic republic centered on a two-house parliament, a supreme court system, and a directly elected presidency; guarantees basic political and civil rights; establishes that women are equal in the eyes of the law; and, in writing at least, squares this with the ideal of Afghanistan being an Islamic Republic with no laws being contrary to Islam.

It is amazing to think that a little more than twenty-three months before President Karzai affixed his signature to this historic document, U.S. and coalition forces were driving the Taliban and al-Qaeda out of their last positions in the mountains of Afghanistan. Although there remains much work to secure Afghanistan against a resurgence of the Taliban, restore its economy, and rebuild its infrastructure, the outlook for Afghanistan is brighter than it has ever been in modern history. This was America's first victory against the Web of Terror. The speed with which the Bush administration organized and executed this counterstroke to the outrage of September 11, 2001, was remarkable. Also remarkable was that this was the first time the United States matched our enemies' militant rhetoric of a global jihad with an equally militant response.

For the terrorists associated with Osama bin Laden's terrorist conglomerate, Afghanistan was a secure base for rest and recuperation, training, recruitment, and money laundering. By September 2001, the al-Qaeda terrorists—Chechens, Arabs, Egyptians, and Pakistanis—were the Taliban's "palace guard." Their arrogant attitude and brutal behavior toward most Afghans made these "Arabs," as the Afghan people referred to them, widely loathed. The interdependence of the Taliban and al-Qaeda meant that the only way to rob al-Qaeda of its sanctuary in Afghanistan was to topple the regime that sheltered it.

Bringing down the Taliban was an obvious goal for other, broader reasons. It set out as a matter of U.S. policy the denial of sanctuaries to terrorists no matter where they were and no matter who gave them protection. Terrorists would know that whether they were in sight of the Hindu Kush or under the jungle canopy of the southern Philippines they would be pursued relentlessly and pitilessly. Governments that gave shelter to terrorists were put on notice: the United States would bring them down.

The first air attacks on the Taliban/al-Qaeda targets in Afghanistan were on October 7, 2001. American diplomats, intelligence personnel on the ground, and Bush administration leaders had paved the way by the diplomatic coup of securing flyover and basing rights in countries bordering Afghanistan—Uzbekistan, Tajikistan, and Pakistan—and receiving permission from many other countries (including the Persian Gulf states of Oman, Bahrain, and Kuwait) to place our forces on their soil. As is so often the case, the Kingdom of Saudi Arabia needed special handling. U.S. Central Command was keen to use the massive Prince Sultan Air Force Base, from which many strikes had flown against Iraq during the 1991 Gulf War. For reasons still unknown, the Saudis declined to allow aircraft to utilize Prince Sultan Air Force Base for strikes against the Taliban and al-Qaeda, but allowed its use as a command-and-control center. As to securing the bases in the Gulf, it was fortunate that Operation Southern Watch (patrolling the southern no-fly zone in Iraq) had been going on for a decade; it had given us invaluable experience in conducting sustained aerial operations at the end of a logistics line many thousands of miles long.

A diplomatic effort that we examined warily was the U.S. government's offer to the Taliban: surrender Osama bin Laden and we will let your regime stand. We were convinced that the Taliban needed to be dealt with, in any event, and we worried that Mullah Omar and others might stall for time while Osama bin Laden and his al-Qaeda command structure escaped. The Taliban, however, made the enormous miscalculation—as did much of world's media—that they could repel a U.S. assault. One media outlet that didn't make that mistake was FOX News Channel, where we were posted as military analysts.

We were grateful for NATO's declaration that the attack on a member country, the United States, demanded a military response. We were grateful that the Vatican lent its moral authority to Operation Enduring Freedom, by endorsing the right of self-defense as applied to the United States against al-Qaeda and the Taliban. We approved the sweeps that law enforcement and internal security organizations made in such countries as France, Germany, Spain, and Italy, actions often based on information provided by the United States.

There was another diplomatic effort, however, that we wish had happened, but didn't, which was for the president to seek a UN Security Council mandate to dismantle the entire Web of Terror. The administration quickly pieced together that the Web existed, that al-Qaeda was an isolated problem. President Bush made this official in his State of the Union speech in 2002 with his identification of the "Axis of Evil." But what would have been even more useful would have been a push in the UN Security Council for a declaration that all state sponsors of terror would be subjects of a possible UN-mandated military response in order to restore international security, law, and peace. There was a precedent for such a declaration, in part at least, with the UN-supported war against North Korean aggression, fifty years earlier. If the United States had pushed for such a resolution in late September

2001, it might very well have passed—as a symbol of moral support if nothing else—and such a resolution might have meant that Saddam Hussein could have been removed as early as the fall of 2002, rather than well into April 2003 after fruitless diplomatic delays.

In our role as military analysts at FOX News Channel, we tried not only to provide strategic and tactical analysis, but to use our military experience to bust some of the myths that civilian reporters fell prey to. When reporters warned about the "harsh Afghan winter," we countered by saying that bad weather cuts both ways and that our forces had superior equipment for moving and fighting in cold weather. Some commentators warned that if we took action against the Taliban and al-Qaeda, thousands of nationalist Afghans would pick up their assault rifles and machine guns, flock to the Taliban's banner, and fight to repel the foreign invaders. We retorted that loyalties in Afghanistan often were more a matter of tribalism than nationalism and that the Taliban and al-Qaeda were widely hated. Many "experts" opined that Afghanistan was an unconquerable land defended by invincible fighters. In reply, we recalled that it had in fact been conquered by the British, the Russians (who withdrew in 1989 only when they decided it wasn't worth the cost), and indeed by the Taliban itself, which was an armed faction that had taken the country, albeit with support from Pakistan's Inter-Service Intelligence (ISI). The courage and fighting prowess of Afghan warriors, often referred to as the mujahideen, was legendary, but the Afghan fighting men were not indestructible—and more important, they were prone to switch sides if it seemed like a good thing to do.

We were not worried about the Taliban and al-Qaeda as a military force—what worried us was how our own generals might approach the task. During his tenure as chairman of the Joint Chiefs of Staff during the late 1980s and 1990s, Colin Powell had articulated "the Powell Doctrine," which had enormous, if unofficial, influence on American military thinking. A central tenet of that "doctrine" was that whenever and wherever the United States sent troops into battle, it had to deploy a numerically overwhelming force. Some compared the doctrine to using a jackhammer to open a walnut, but to others, the Persian Gulf War of 1991 with its "100 Hour War" on the ground seemed to bear out Powell's vision.

In our experience, if an Army general (and not a few Marine generals) were asked what constitutes "overwhelming force," he would describe a heavy mechanized force—tanks, armored fighting vehicles, and self-propelled artillery. Moving U.S. Army divisions, even light ones, into a landlocked, mountainous country would be cutting out a massive piece of work for the Army and other services.

Initially, this massive force would have to move almost entirely by air. The power of Islamist political parties in Pakistan being what they were—and are—moving it across that country by land would have been asking the government of General Pervez Musharraf (still a largely unknown character) to take an enormous political risk. Considering that the Taliban and al-Qaeda were active in the provinces that bordered Afghanistan and had recruited young men to fight for them from the *madrassas* of those regions, any U.S. force moving through those provinces would have had enormous security problems and an unsecured supply line.

Moving heavy forces by air, however, is notoriously inefficient. The only transport aircraft capable of lifting the Army's 72-ton M-1 Abrams tank are the C-5A and C-17. Even if the way had been cleared to move the equipment sets of three divisions to Turkey by sea, before transporting them to the Incirlik air base in northern Turkey by land, and then moving them by air, deploying a force that large would have taken months. Equipment cannot just be dumped on the ground; it must be maintained, armed, and fueled, and that means maintenance facilities, fuel depots, and ammunition dumps must be established. Advanced communications networks and headquarters facilities are essential to wage modern warfare. Although there were some old Soviet bases in such places as Uzbekistan, the United States military would have had to establish modern facilities by building them from scratch. Even if the forces began arriving in late September 2001, there would be little chance for the force to begin operations before the spring of 2002.

In the time that the buildup was going on, the Taliban might have received more aid from Pakistan's ISI, or successfully appealed to portions of the Islamic world for support, or kept an invasion on hold by surrendering a few low-level al-Qaeda fighters and offering protracted negotiations.

Although we were later told that General Franks had indeed recommended to the president and the secretary of defense that the United States go into Afghanistan with three divisions (President Bush and Secretary Rumsfeld immediately rejected the idea), we took comfort from one piece of information making the rounds of the Washington grapevine: the president wanted action *now*. In turn, we knew that he would not be willing to wait the months necessary to move and position a force that size into Afghanistan. As September drifted into October, we knew that U.S. naval forces were moving to the Arabian Sea, which meant strike aircraft from U.S. aircraft carriers and U.S. Marines would be available to Central Command. U.S. military aircraft began deploying to the Persian Gulf, and a one-thousand-man force of the 10th Mountain Division was designated for dispatch to Uzbekistan, presumably to guard the air bases there. We assumed that U.S. satellites were examining every possible inch of Afghanistan and U.S. special operations forces probably were in bases in Uzbekistan, Tajikistan, and Pakistan and entering Afghanistan to conduct reconnaissance and talk to locals. Still, we figured it would be a few weeks before any force that would have any chance of success in Afghanistan would be ready.

THE AIR CAMPAIGN

When the air strikes began on Sunday, October 7, 2001, we were pleased. The necessary blow was being struck—swiftly and surely— on a schedule even better than we had hoped.

The air campaign began with strikes by cruise missiles fired from U.S. Navy warships; heavy bombers flying from the "unsinkable aircraft carrier," the island of Diego Garcia; and U.S. Navy strike aircraft from U.S. aircraft carriers. Two days later, the air strikes began in broad daylight; on October 11, the initial target list was complete. The bombing had destroyed the Afghan air-defense missile system, the remnants of the Afghan air force, heavy equipment (such as tanks), and the Afghan telephone system. The Taliban now had no way of knocking down U.S. aircraft except by handheld antiaircraft missiles, antiaircraft artillery, and machine guns and little left in the way to counter lighter ground forces. The demise of the telephone system forced the Taliban and al-Qaeda to use radio and cellular telephones for communication—both of which were susceptible to interception, jamming, and surveillance. After the initial list of targets was hit, coalition air power ranged everywhere over Afghanistan, chasing the Taliban and dismantling other parts of the Taliban's military power—in other words, preparing the battlefield for the ground offensive to come.

One problem with the air campaign, however, was its desultory pace. Certainly, the coalition aircraft were hitting their targets, but for the first couple of weeks, the aircraft were restricted to those that came "from the sea" from U.S. aircraft carriers in the Arabian Sea and the Gulf of Oman, from U.S. Air Force heavy bombers (B-52s and B-1s) from Diego Garcia, and on occasion from B-2 "Spirit" bombers flying round trips from their bases in Missouri to Afghanistan and back without landing. Moreover, almost every aircraft involved needed aerial refueling support, and this significantly stressed our tanker force, which is moving into bloc obsolescence. It was clear that there was a compelling need to modernize our aerial tanker force.

In Operation Enduring Freedom, General Franks chose to use advanced communications technology to exercise his command from the headquarters of U.S. Central Command at MacDill Air Force Base in Tampa, Florida. As "gee-whiz" as that was, separating a theater commander, especially one who is expected to exercise day-to-day *command,* not just provide general guidance, from the forces he is supposed to command is asking for trouble. So it turned out to be in Operation Enduring Freedom. During the air campaign, Central Command often refused to delegate decisions about hitting targets; all questions about whether or not to strike at a target were referred back to Central Command. This disrupted what the Air Force refers to as "time critical targeting," in which a target of opportunity presents itself and there is limited time to act on it. Too often during the air campaign, there were targets that could have—and should have—been struck, but the authorization to do so was not immediately available. Often, too, the rules of engagement were too restrictive, and because of them, opportunities were lost.

There were at least two "opportunities lost" to hit the leader of the Taliban, Mullah Omar. On the first night of the war, a CIA-controlled armed Predator unmanned aerial vehicle, armed with two Hellfire antitank missiles, spotted a convoy in which Mullah Omar was said to be traveling. It would have been simple for the UAV operator to fire the missiles at the convoy and perhaps kill the top man in the Taliban. The rules of engagement for the CIA, however, were such that the operator had to ask for permission to fire. The aerial images and permission request were forwarded to U.S. Central Command; there, a *military lawyer* made the decision *not* to fire.

Another time, Mullah Omar was tracked to a building in Afghanistan. A strike package was hastily put together to hit the target. But an analyst—looking at the images streaming in from the UAV circling the building—spotted a tall, cylindrical structure nearby. Was it a minaret or a chimney or something else? The rules of engagement forbid the deliberate targeting of mosques. While those looking at the streaming video from the image tried to figure out if the building was a mosque or a factory, Mullah Omar made his escape. There should have been some clear delegation of authority *downward,* some recognition that "trigger-pullers" need an immediate response on manhunts, and that the answers as cleared by bureaucrats and lawyers aren't always the best ones.

Another problem with the initial air campaign was that it was somewhat misdirected. The destruction of the Taliban's air defenses and communications facilities made sense, but afterward, the need to pummel other fixed, preselected targets seemed less pressing. When someone remarked that the U.S. aerial campaign was an attempt to bomb the Taliban back into the Stone Age, Paul retorted by saying, "They are already *in* the Stone Age." The serious point to be made was that the air campaign should have been quickly redirected to destroying military units rather than fixed sites. The combined forces air component commander (CFACC) wanted a far more aggressive air campaign but was restricted initially by the CENTCOM staff.

THE COLLAPSE OF THE TALIBAN

Why did the widely feared Taliban collapse so quickly in the fall of 2001, so quickly in fact that in less than two months, it was driven out of its cultural capital of Kandahar and over the border to Pakistan? The answer is coordinated American firepower delivered from the air and on the ground. Both elements were crucial. The Clinton administration had made a habit of relying purely on symbolic air strikes when it wanted to deploy military power. But to win an objective it takes more than air strikes, it takes soldiers on the ground. And Operation Enduring Freedom as it was actually employed got the balance exactly right, using American and indigenous forces, including rapidly deployable units—Special Forces and Marines—U.S. airpower (lots of it), and the Afghan Northern Alliance.

The U.S. Army's Special Forces—popularly known as the "Green Berets"—have long had the mission of raising, training, and leading indigenous forces. In Southeast Asia, they organized the mountain tribes of Vietnam's Central Highlands, "the Montagnards," into special operations forces to battle units of the North Vietnamese Army and the

Viet Cong. In Afghanistan, the Green Berets, and their colleagues in the CIA, prepared the Northern Alliance for a far grander job—liberating their entire country. It worked because of U.S. airpower. The Special Forces acted as the "eyes" of that airpower, using advanced targeting technology, such as laser designators, that could guide precision weapons, or "smart bombs," to targets. The Special Forces' presence also indicated that the Americans were *committed* to the defeat of the Taliban and al-Qaeda and that we shared a common combat bond with the Afghans.

On September 11, 2001, the Northern Alliance held only 10 percent of the country. By October 20, 2001, three U.S. Special Forces "A-teams" had entered Afghanistan—their paths prepared and their welcomes arranged by CIA agents—and were in contact with the Northern Alliance commanders (two A-teams were inserted around Mazar-i-Sharif; another was with Northern Alliance forces near Kabul). In one week's time, the Green Berets had honed the skills of Alliance soldiers, demonstrated to them the usefulness of their targeting equipment, and used it to bring "smart bombs" onto Taliban positions (as well as some "dumb" ones from B-52s). The effect of the heavy bombing was devastating to the Taliban defenders. So impressed were they with the ability of the Americans to put bombs apparently anywhere they wished that the Taliban referred to U.S. targeting equipment, the laser designators especially, as "the death ray." The combination of accurate, heavy bombing and a motivated ground force was sufficient to drive the Taliban out of Mazar-i-Sharif on November 9, 2001. For the forces around Kabul, the combination worked its magic as well: by November 12, Northern Alliance forces had entered Kabul (as well as captured two other important cities in the western and northeastern parts of Afghanistan). Two days later, the Taliban had fled the capital, retreating toward the Afghanistan-Pakistan border or toward the city of Kandahar.

In mid-November, a Green Beret A-team joined up with the Pushtun leader Hamid Karzai (now Afghanistan's president) in the southern part of Afghanistan near the city of Kandahar. On November 25, after a bold movement in which they leapfrogged from amphibious ships in the Arabian Sea to Pakistani airfields and thence to an abandoned airfield south of Kandahar, several hundred U.S. Marines entered the battle. After establishing their camp, they fanned out searching for Taliban, al-Qaeda, and weapons dumps. On December 6, the city of Kandahar fell to Pushtun fighters recruited by Karzai and supported by the Green Berets and U.S. airpower. Thus, in two months, the Taliban and al-Qaeda were driven out of every major city in Afghanistan.

This victory could have been achieved sooner if Central Command had listened to its component commanders in the area of operations and attacked the Taliban and al-Qaeda forces occupying these cities within the first week of the campaign. This would have shortened the campaign significantly. Unfortunately, the Special Forces A-teams were not inserted prior to the beginning of hostilities and General Franks' staff was conducting a classic campaign versus a modern campaign of blitz warfare.

SECURING THE VICTORY?

As broadly satisfying as these victories in Afghanistan were, there was still work to do, especially in the areas along the Pakistan-Afghanistan border. Intelligence—and rumor—indicated that the surviving "Arabs," meaning Osama bin Laden and other members of al-Qaeda, had gone to ground in a complex of caves in the Tora Bora mountains in eastern Afghanistan. U.S. Central Command decided to mount an operation to dig these al-Qaeda fighters out of the caves, killing or capturing them.

When it came to capturing Osama bin Laden and his terrorists, Central Command made a mistake. Instead of using the one thousand men of the 10th Mountain Division or redirecting the Marines in Afghanistan onto the mission, General Franks decided to apply the same formula in this fight that had been so successful in other places in Afghanistan: Afghan fighters backed by U.S. Special Forces and supported by U.S. airpower. For a blocking force, Central Command depended on Pakistani border units, not American ones. While the Tora Bora battles undoubtedly led to the deaths of hundreds of al-Qaeda terrorists, the "big fish"—to include Osama bin Laden—escaped. With so much at stake, the blocking force straddling the Afghanistan-Pakistan border should have been an American or mixed coalition force; that way, General Franks would have been sure that a strong effort was made to shut the back door out of Afghanistan and trap as many al-Qaeda as possible between two forces

Beginning in March 2002, Operation Anaconda was the last "main force" action of Operation Enduring Freedom and the first one to use large numbers of more "conventional" soldiers—the 10th Mountain Division and the 101st Airborne (Air Assault) Division as well as a broad variety of special operations forces, drawn from different countries. While we were glad to see some of the U.S. Army's larger units involved in the fight in Afghanistan, there was considerable "friction" between the Army and the Air Force during this bold winter offensive against al-Qaeda enclaves. There were also some hairy moments when a few of the landing zones for airmobile assaults ended up being right under the noses of al-Qaeda and Taliban fighters. This was caused by lack of coordination between the 10th Mountain Division commander with the CFACC. Fortunately, the lessons learned during Anaconda were applied in Operation Iraqi Freedom with great success.

Although we had some objections to the initial plans and the conduct of the final phases of the campaign, we agreed that, overall, Operation Enduring Freedom had been a huge success. The Taliban had been broken and al-Qaeda routed. The president and his national security team had demonstrated strength and resolve. And the U.S. military had executed an extraordinarily swift and effective strike from an extraordinary distance and shown far more creative thinking than it is usually given credit for.

With Operation Enduring Freedom, special operations forces had truly entered into a new era, combining their traditional missions with a new one of acting as the "eyes-on-the-ground" for precision air-power. The Navy proved that though the battlefield was landlocked and many hundreds of miles from any ocean, our aircraft carriers and their embarked aircraft could be a crucial component of the air campaign in Afghanistan. The Navy flew more than 70 percent of all combat sorties. Yet, thanks to the participation of the Air Force's heavy bomber fleet in the air campaign, the Air Force dropped 80 percent of the bombs used. The B-1s, B-2s, and B-52s were capable of dropping up to twenty-four precision-guided bombs per aircraft. While we could have used more aerial refueling aircraft, another aerial improvement was the introduction of various unmanned aerial vehicles that provided unparalleled aerial reconnaissance. And the effectiveness of America's "boots on the ground" trigger-pullers—Army, Navy SEALs, and Marines—showed what a few good men can truly do. Watching our victory in Afghanistan was a proud and glorious experience, but we knew that this was only the beginning.

CHAPTER FIVE

NOTES FROM A CAMPAIGN OF LIBERATION: IRAQ

A FTER THE SUCCESS OF Operation Enduring Freedom in Afghanistan, some analysts suggested that with al-Qaeda effectively scattered, the United States should return to the law enforcement paradigm of counterterrorism. Others insisted that the United States should follow its victory in Afghanistan with an effort to bring peace between the Israelis and the Palestinians, or between India and Pakistan. But we knew these strategies wouldn't work; they were the outdated strategies of previous administrations. For eight years, the Clinton administration treated terrorism as a law-enforcement matter and focused on the "peace process" in the Middle East. During those same eight years, al-Qaeda gained in strength and audacity, escalating its attacks on American targets until the events of September 11. Based on experience, that is no model for preventing and defeating terrorism.

On February 22, 2002, we left the Washington, D.C., studios of FOX News Channel for a working lunch at the restaurant La Colline, during which we sketched out the campaign against our next selected target in the war on terror: Saddam Hussein. Why did we think Saddam Hussein should be next? Saddam Hussein compared himself to the medieval Muslim hero Saladin—ironically, a Kurd—and his ambitions ran to the creation of a "Greater Iraq" that would gobble up large portions of Iraq's neighbors or, as in the case of Kuwait, swallow them whole and become the dominant power in the Middle East. To that end, he invaded Iran in 1980, and fought the Iranians for eight years. He invaded Kuwait in 1990. It was after his ouster from Kuwait that we discovered just how far advanced was his effort to build a nuclear bomb.

In the aftermath of the 1991 Gulf War, international inspectors dismantled Saddam Hussein's chemical, biological, and nuclear weapons programs, but the trained personnel necessary for reconstituting those weapons remained, as did Saddam Hussein's ambitions to build these weapons and, based on his insatiable desire for cash, become a proliferator of weapons of mass destruction.

Saddam Hussein's Iraq kept bad company—as one might expect of a regime that practiced mass executions, torture, and arbitrary arrest and imprisonment and used chemical weapons against its own people. Iraq had extensive dealings with terrorists. Two Palestinians at the top of many terrorism-related "most wanted" lists in the 1980s and the 1990s—Abu Nidal (real name: Sabri al-Banna) and Abu Abbas—were given sanctuary by Saddam Hussein. Abu Nidal led an organization that committed a number of bloody attacks in Europe, the Middle East, and South Asia. Abu Abbas masterminded the 1985 hijacking of the cruise ship the *Achille Lauro,* a crime that included the murder of a wheelchair-bound American passenger. Iraq provided training camps for terrorists, most notoriously at Salman Pak, south of Baghdad, where an obsolescent Boeing 707 was used to train terrorists to hijack airliners. Iraq made cash payments to the families of Palestinian suicide bombers. Saddam Hussein's vice president, Taha Yasin Ramadan, was specifically tasked with supporting the terrorist activities of the PLO, Hamas, and Palestinian Islamic Jihad. The Iraqis had tried to assassinate President George H. W. Bush. Iraq had ties to al-Qaeda, as was reported by both Sudanese and Czechoslovakian intelligence. In addition, the al-Qaeda affiliate, Ansar al-Islam, was based in northern Iraq, where it was a potentially destabilizing influence on Kurdish opposition groups.

Saddam Hussein's combined sins of massive human rights violations, state support of international terrorism, and development and
use of weapons of mass destruction made his removal our first priority after Operation Enduring Freedom. Some people suggested that the
best option vis-à-vis Iraq was to continue the de facto containment
policy of the 1990s. We rejected that idea for a number of reasons.
First, Iraq had subverted the sanctions through illegal means with the
cooperation of regimes like Syria. Second, international support for
maintaining the sanctions was wavering. Third, we knew that French,
German, and Russian businesses continued to fuel Saddam Hussein's
illegal weapons programs. There was every reason to believe that Saddam Hussein would develop—or had already stockpiled—weapons of
mass destruction; every intelligence agency in the world agreed on
that point. And it was reasonable to believe, especially given the Iraqi
attempt to assassinate former president George H. W. Bush, that Saddam Hussein might provide such weapons, covertly and with plausible deniability, to a terrorist organization to strike the United States.
After September 11, 2001, we weren't willing to take that risk.

A few days earlier, Tom had appeared on FOX News Channel's
Special Report with Brit Hume with Dennis Ross, former special
ambassador to the Middle East during both the Bush and Clinton
administrations. After the show, he asked Ambassador Ross what sig-
nificance a "lightning campaign" that brought down Saddam Hussein
in less than thirty days would have politically. Ambassador Ross
replied that since most Arab governments held Saddam Hussein in
utter contempt, the only potential source of objection would be the
suffering of the Iraqi people if the campaign dragged out into a slugfest
lasting for months. If the United States could topple Saddam Hussein
in less than thirty days, he said, the reaction of Arab governments
would be limited to muted pro forma objections.

After we had counted off the reasons for getting rid of Saddam Hussein, therefore, Tom's first question to Paul was "Could the Army execute a thirty-day ground campaign?" Almost immediately, Paul

replied in the affirmative. We then got to work on the general outlines of the campaign, "a war of liberation," using a paper napkin to do so.

The center of gravity of the regime was not the Iraqi army but the government in Baghdad. In our plan, therefore, allied forces would drive to Baghdad from three directions—the north, west, and south, with possible jumping off points in Turkey, Saudi Arabia (or possibly Jordan), and Kuwait. We agreed that with the right tactics and techniques, victory could be achieved in less than thirty days, with a force smaller than that used in the 1991 Gulf War (we estimated that eleven or twelve brigades or 100,000-plus U.S. troops—not counting coalition and Iraqi opposition forces—could do the job), and with relatively few allied and Iraqi casualties.

The important element in this campaign would be the manner of its execution. For that, we embraced the concept of "blitz warfare"—a simultaneous and ferocious assault by air power and fast-moving conventional ground forces and special operations forces—all married to the most advanced information technology. Since we conceived this campaign as one of liberation, Iraqi freedom fighters were an important element of the force. Based on our conversations with members of the Iraqi National Congress and high-ranking Iraqi exiles, we estimated that as many as ten thousand Iraqis could be recruited and trained in time for the campaign.

THE THIRTY-DAY TAKEDOWN

We knew the oil fields had to be seized early to avoid an environmental catastrophe like the one Iraq attempted to create in Kuwait in 1991 and to ensure that the new government of Iraq would have sufficient economic resources. Likewise, neutralizing any Iraqi missile threat was a top priority. The major objectives, however, were to isolate and decapitate the regime's command and control and knock out the regime's underpinnings by defeating in detail the military and security units that kept Saddam Hussein's regime secure in its position of power. The Iraqi army did not, in our estimate, need to be destroyed entirely. Defeat the regime's command and control, we thought, defeat those units most loyal to Saddam Hussein, and the remaining Iraqi conscripts would fade away rather than fight for their oppressor.

As we sketched out the plan's outline, we were mindful of its logistical demands, and we factored in shifts required by politics, domestic and international. After a couple of weeks of discussing and adjusting the details of the plan, we mentioned it to Bill O'Reilly at the FOX News Channel party before the annual TV and Radio Banquet in Washington, D.C. After we laid out for him our "War of Liberation" strategy in very broad terms, he booked us for the next evening's show. We knew appearing on *The O'Reilly Factor* to discuss the plan was something of a risk. In the past, we had acted solely as military *analysts*. Presenting our plan came close to *advocacy*. But having stuck our necks out on Bill's show, we did it again the following week, when Paul appeared on *FOX and Friends* promoting the idea of a "war of liberation" that could be won in thirty days.

Both of us have worked with the Pentagon and the Congress, and we knew our plan would receive a mixed reaction. Pentagon planners and members of Congress were relatively cautious. Some "think tank" critics thought we were overselling the capabilities of our armed forces. Their caution, their doubts didn't sway us. Throughout the rest of the winter and well into the summer and fall of 2002, we promoted a "war of liberation" that could be achieved through the application of "blitz warfare." Tom did so in print in an op-ed in the *Wall Street Journal* and in testimony to both the Senate Armed Services Committee and Senate Foreign Relations Committee. We did so as well, in numerous meetings in Washington, D.C., and during our appearances on FOX News Channel. We knew we were making headway. Eventually, the words "War of Liberation" began filtering out in press conferences and materials from the Department of Defense, the State Department, and the White House. By the time Congress reconvened in September 2002, members of the Department of Defense were asking us for practical details of our plan and inquiring as to how we had come by our estimates of Iraqi morale and other factors.

When we asked why the Pentagon—the paid experts who were drawing up the real plans—was asking us, retired generals, for the details of *our* plan, we were told that, insofar as a campaign against Iraq was concerned, the Pentagon had initially envisaged "Desert Storm II," a massive operation with as many as *eight divisions and 500,000 troops.* After Operation Enduring Freedom, however, Secretary Rumsfeld, General Franks, and other leaders in the Defense Department had come to believe that a smaller joint force backed by air power and supported by special operations forces could liberate Iraq. So we confirmed two things: first, that the Pentagon was planning the liberation of Iraq; and second, that our message resonated within the upper echelons of the Defense Department.

We were surprised at how many liberal commentators and Democratic politicians opposed the liberation of Iraq. We had assumed there was bipartisan agreement on this point. After all, President Clinton had ordered strikes against some of Saddam Hussein's facilities for building and storing weapons of mass destruction in Operation Desert Fox in 1998, without United Nations approval. In 1998, Congress had passed the Iraqi Liberation Act by an overwhelming majority, which made "regime change" in Iraq the official policy of the United States. Still, we heard many fervent arguments against the liberation of Iraq among them:

"The liberation of Iraq will overstretch the American military."

While it was true the U.S. military was conducting operations at a tempo unmatched since the 1991 Persian Gulf War, deploying four to five infantry divisions and a reinforced Marine Expeditionary Force plus air and naval forces—a combined operations total of roughly 250,000 troops—to Iraq would not overstretch a military that had more than a million in active-duty personnel.

"The liberation of Iraq will distract us from the war on terror."

There were two ill-founded ideas behind this objection. The first stemmed from a narrow definition of terrorism—that is, outside al-Qaeda there is no terrorism. It is true that Saddam Hussein was not as active in supporting terrorists as Iran and Libya, but he was still a blatant state sponsor of terror, and knocking him over was not a diversion from the fight against the Web of Terror, but an integral part of it, especially since his defeat would deny terrorists one source of weapons of mass destruction. The second wrong idea was that the United States couldn't chew gum and walk at the same time: that is, we couldn't fight al-Qaeda and Iraq at the same time. The fact is, we could and we did.

"Iraq will use chemical and biological weapons against our forces."

We could never quite understand why this was supposed to be a "showstopper." Admittedly, operating in a chemical or biological environment is at once cumbersome and dangerous. However, that is why the U.S. military has put so much money into countermeasures—from chemical warfare suits for soldiers to filtration systems for vehicles—as well as chemical and biological reconnaissance capabilities. Moreover, chemical and biological weapons are "equal opportunity" weapons; an attack using, say, mustard gas can harm the forces that use the weapon; all it takes is a shift in wind. We were confident that given the state of the Iraqi army in late 2002, if Iraq used these weapons they might prove to be more dangerous to the Iraqi army than to ours.

"Baghgrad."

Another argument against the liberation of Iraq was that even if the campaign were initially successful in defeating the Iraqi army, it would bog down in the streets of the Iraqi capital. The Special Republican Guard and other forces would turn Baghdad into an updated version of Stalingrad, a bloody house-by-house battle that would cause thousands of American casualties and tens of thousands of Iraqi casualties and might even lead to the defeat of the U.S. forces. This was a legitimate concern—and the very reason why we stressed the need to adopt a plan for a swift campaign using overwhelming firepower and focused on toppling the regime. We also had human intelligence that no fortifications were being built in Baghdad; the Republican Guards were not training for urban warfare; and no Republican Guard divisions were being allowed into Baghdad (because Saddam Hussein feared they might launch a coup). Finally, if there had been a siege of Baghdad, American tactics would have made it a very different scenario than what happened at Stalingrad. We were confident that house-to-house fighting would not be necessary to win such a battle. Our confidence stemmed from our knowledge that the combined forces air component commander (CFACC) had been developed and trained for "urban close air support" at Nellis Air Force Base. Centered on the use of precision munitions striking at regime targets, it would have broken the back of any major, organized resistance and prevented the nightmarish "Baghgrad" scenario from happening.

Civilian Casualties.

Every war kills people who are not in uniform. But we argued—and Afghanistan showed—that joint operations that combine precision guided weaponry and special operations forces, while not perfectly safe, minimize civilian casualties—more so than ever before. The campaign we planned was designed to shield civilians by achieving quick results and by focusing on the regime that held the Iraqi people captive to a ruthless tyrant, rather than waging a massive "total war." Again, based on the experience in Operation Enduring Freedom, we knew that every possible safeguard to prevent civilian casualties would be in place. The risk of civilian casualties was more than outweighed by the reward of a successful campaign: freeing the Iraqi people from a dictator whose deliberately and systematically conducted mass executions of his political opponents, real and perceived. In the end, the moral calculus favored action against Saddam Hussein. All postwar polls show that the Iraqi people hold the same view.

"The Recruiting Sergeant for Terrorism."

Opponents of the war predicted the Iraq campaign would drive more young men into the ranks of terrorist organizations. Our response was that the campaign might lead to a short-term spurt of public support for Saddam Hussein, but that not many young men would be motivated to join an Islamic terrorist group in order to avenge a disgraced dictator whose appeal was not to radical Islamism, but to Arab nationalism, an ideology held in contempt by many radical Islamists. And which is the better recruiter—the Ba'ath Party successfully thumbing its nose at the United States, or Saddam Hussein captured or dead, his mass graves and corruption exposed, and Iraqis cheering their liberation?

The Arab Street.

This mythical beast haunts the dreams and waking thoughts of many responsible journalists, editorialists, legislators, academics, and government officials. When angered, it is, allegedly, a fearsome creature, lashing out indiscriminately, wreaking havoc, and devouring whole governments. Of course what the "Arab street" really amounts to is footage for the nightly news—and no more than that.

Free Iraqi Forces.

Another thing that perplexed us, aside from liberal and Democratic opposition to liberating Iraq, was the inattention of the administration to Iraqi resistance organizations, including the Iraqi National Congress. The State Department, CIA, and Defense Department all had their various reasons and excuses for not dealing with or adequately supporting the Iraqi exiles, but we found these excuses unconvincing.

We say this while well knowing the dangers of émigré organizations. Often they can be much more effective at soliciting money from the U.S. government than achieving any results in their home country. Another danger is that these organizations can be fronts for or penetrated by spies.

When Paul accepted an invitation to meet with the head of the Washington office of the Iraqi National Congress, Entifadh Qanbar, a former Iraqi air force captain, he was directed to an address not on K Street or Connecticut Avenue or any other high-priced location, but approximately ten blocks from the Capitol, off Pennsylvania Avenue, Southeast. There, Paul found a two-story row house, unmarked with any sign indicating the INC's presence. Mr. Qanbar explained that it was from this house that he and his small staff ran the INC's entire U.S. effort. This was an organization that preferred doing hard work to luxuriating in plush offices.

The INC Washington staff gathered information on the Iraqi government—largely from American-based Iraqi defectors with relatives still living in Iraq—and passed it on to the INC's London headquarters for analysis. At the INC's London office, analysts combined that information with the information that the INC received from sources in the Middle East (including some brave agents operating in Iraq) and Europe. They, in turn, sent the combined analyzed intelligence to Mr. Qanbar, who passed it on to his contacts in the U.S. Defense Intelligence Agency.

Mr. Qanbar told Paul that though the INC had a lead role in pushing the Iraq Liberation Act through Congress—which had made regime change the official policy of the U.S. government—the INC had received only $5 million of a promised $97 million from a grudging State Department and CIA. The Pentagon, however, had proved friendlier, and it was through the Department of Defense that he had established decent ties with the Defense Intelligence Agency.

Mr. Qanbar took Paul down the street to a second house that served as the repository of information on the Iraqi regime, including its military, intelligence service, and internal security organizations, which the INC had worked into an exceptionally detailed order-of-battle. There were also organizational charts and lists of Iraqi officers and

civil servants, complete with their assignments, addresses, and telephone numbers, as well as, in many cases, their cellular telephone
numbers and their e-mail addresses. The files were extensive, up-to-
date, and, from what we knew of the Iraqi military from other
sources, accurate.

What made the INC even more impressive to Paul was that Mr.
Qanbar made no exaggerated claims for the INC or for the information
it had gathered. In fact, Mr. Qanbar said that the INC was frustrated by
what it still *didn't know* about the regime. The INC had no reliable
source in the upper echelon of the Ba'ath Party or Iraqi intelligence
and, although some of the more recent defectors were men of high
rank, Saddam Hussein's fetish for security meant that they brought out
little information of lasting value on the higher levels of the Iraqi government. Another gap the INC admitted to concerned Iraq's weapons
of mass destruction; there was little recent information on the location
of any weapons and the status of the programs.

Why did this make the INC more credible? Look at it this way. The
information that was most prized by the coalition in the run-up to the
campaign against Saddam Hussein was information about the upper
echelon of the Iraqi government and Iraq's WMD programs. If the INC
had wanted to garner attention and money from the U.S. government,
it could have touted its information as the final word on these topics
and hinted that, yes, it had highly placed sources in the Iraqi WMD
program and at the very top of the Iraqi government. The INC chose
not to make those claims, because they were not true.

During the next few months, our contacts with the INC grew
stronger. Not long after Paul's meeting with Mr. Qanbar, the INC
invited Tom to meet the staff and look at the information that the INC
had on file. He came away impressed not only by what he had read,
but also by the overall tone of the operation.

During the next few months, our opinion of the INC became even
more positive. The information they provided to us compared favor-
ably with that we received from other sources. We became aware of

just how extensive their networks were, reaching across the United States, Europe, and the Middle East. Through the INC, we met many high-level defectors from Ba'athist Iraq—including Khidir Hamza, a nuclear scientist widely known as "Saddam's Bomb-maker." He gave us excellent insight into the situation in Iraq and allowed us to set new information we had gathered into proper perspective. The INC's sources, leaders, and staff members struck us as well educated, well informed, and sincerely committed to the overthrow of the Ba'athist regime and the establishment of a democratic state in its stead. They were also mindful of the work that would be necessary to carry out both these aims.

Just as important as this information, however, was the INC's willingness to serve in Operation Iraqi Freedom. Its members wanted to help the allied coalition forces by offering intelligence and information that only an Iraqi national would know. Almost from the beginning of our relationship, the INC told us that they had no shortage of volunteers who would accompany our forces into the field, and help with everything from acting as translators to assisting with psychological operations.

We tried to interest administration officials in taking up the INC's offers of assistance. Tom recommended that a senior Iraqi general who was working with the INC, General Najeb al Salhi, be attached to U.S. Central Command as an advisor. We also recommended that small teams of trained Iraqi émigrés (drawn from all legitimate groups) be attached to frontline battalions and companies. The members of these teams would act as interpreters, translators, and guides; aid in intelligence work and prisoner interrogation; help with psychological and information operations; and serve as the point of contact with local Iraqis. After hostilities ended, these volunteers would be invaluable to any civil affairs effort.

Our suggestions and others for using the Iraqi émigrés went for naught, however, until late 2002, when Secretary Rumsfeld took the INC completely under the wing of the Defense Department. He ordered a program to recruit and train Iraqi volunteers. Approximately three thousand Iraqis were eventually recruited, assembled at an air base in Hungary, and formed into the Free Iraqi Forces (FIF). Unfortunately, the majority of these forces were not used and their talents, their language skills, and their local area knowledge were not taken advantage of by Central Command's planners. This was a major mistake.

Although the Pentagon finally came around to the need to utilize the INC and the FIF, the effort proved to be ultimately disappointing. Entifadh Qanbar was eventually assigned to the U.S. Central Command headquarters. In late March, U.S. C-130s flew six hundred of the Free Iraq Forces to an air base near An Nasiriyah and, from there, they hooked up with U.S. units headed toward Baghdad. They performed well, but had the Pentagon created a larger force earlier (like the 10,000-member force we had suggested) and placed them with the coalition forces well *before* the invasion of Iraq began, they would have been much more effective.

The 4th Infantry Division.

The 4th Infantry Division was another underutilized asset. It has performed magnificently in the counterinsurgency war in Iraq, its crowning achievement being the capture of Saddam Hussein in December 2003. Few might remember it now, but immediately before Operation Iraqi Freedom, it was doubtful that this unit of 17,000 soldiers would even participate in the campaign.

Dubbed the "Digital Division," the 4th Infantry Division has a place of pride in the Army as its most technologically advanced fighting unit. Under the plan the Pentagon drew up, ships carrying the 4th Infantry Division's equipment would have landed in Turkey, the unit's soldiers, who had flown ahead to meet the ships, then would have unloaded their equipment, and the division then would have moved overland through Turkey and the Kurd-held areas in northern Iraq before driving south toward Baghdad. It was to be the anvil for the forces driving up from the south led by the 3rd ID. This would have enabled the coalition forces to defeat the Iraqi forces in about twelve to fourteen days. But it was not to be.

In January 2003, however, the Turkish parliament—under an arcane parliamentary rule—rejected the landing and the transit of the 4th Infantry Division. With the 4th Infantry Division effectively withdrawn from the order-of-battle, U.S. Central Command now had no way to cut the Damascus-Baghdad road, a route taken by jihadists, arms smugglers, and, as we were later informed by reliable sources, Iraqi weapons of mass destruction on their way to be hidden in Syria and the Bekaa Valley, where we believe they are now.

Without the 4th Infantry Division driving down from Turkey, U.S. commanders were limited to deploying special operations forces and whatever Kurdish forces they could muster to move south toward Mosul and Kirkuk and to the west near Syria. The problem was that their mobility would be limited and they could not bring much firepower to bear beyond that which coalition airpower provided. Thus, Saddam Hussein would have been free to move forces to the south to face the deep penetration attacks of the Army and Marines.

It has been widely reported—for example, by Oliver North in his excellent book on the campaign, *War Stories: Operation Iraqi Freedom*—that General Tommy Franks, the head of Central Command, decided to use the 4th Infantry Division as a strategic deception. He did not order the ships carrying the division's equipment to rush through the Suez Canal and around to the Persian Gulf. Instead, he held the ships off the Turkish coast, giving the Iraqi army the impression that a secret deal was in the works to deploy the 4th Infantry Division to the northern front. Apparently, this ruse worked and some of Saddam Hussein's army held their positions north of Baghdad until it was too late to attempt to save the regime. However, they never had a chance from the very beginning against this magnificent combined air, land, and sea force.

Central Command eventually did open up a "northern front" with the 173rd Airborne Brigade. After linking with the special operations forces and Kurdish forces in the area, the Brigade moved southward toward Mosul, Kirkuk, and other cities in the northern region and essentially was a fixing force, as it was too light to be decisive.

Initially, it could have been different. When we put forth the plan for war of liberation, we suggested a force coming into northern Iraq via the Kurdish areas and Turkey. We did not, however, envision a force as heavy or as large as the 4th Infantry Division doing that particular job, but rather a lighter force such as a brigade of the 101st Airborne Division using indigenous Iraqi forces such as the Kurds. This force would have had a smaller footprint in Turkey and yet would have packed more punch and mobility than the 173rd Brigade's paratroopers.

It still perplexes us that, knowing the political situation in Turkey, the Bush administration did not try to move a smaller, lighter force through Turkey rather than the almost 80,000-strong force proposed. Without question this large force would have achieved the swift decisive results that General Franks desired. However, given Turkey's enduring stand against terrorism, the Turkish prime minister and his cabinet might have approved the passage of a smaller unit, much as Jordan apparently allowed special operations forces to carry out their work from airfields in that country. In any case, the flexibility exhibited by General Franks's forces was extraordinary.

THE REAL TAKEDOWN:
OPERATION IRAQI FREEDOM

Operation Iraqi Freedom was a resounding victory for the coalition and an amazing achievement of American arms. As we write this chapter, we are fast approaching the campaign's first anniversary and, with the dust raised by the campaign now all but settled, it seems a good time to evaluate it in order to determine what it demonstrated about how we will fight in the twenty-first century.

No Sanctuaries:

Like Operation Enduring Freedom, the campaign in Iraq stakes out an important grand strategic principle: if you are part of the Web of Terror, if you sponsor, support, and conduct terrorism or pursue weapons of mass destruction, count yourself part of the Axis of Evil, and the United States and its allies will reserve the option of taking you out.

Actionable Intelligence:

For commanders at any level, actionable intelligence is, to borrow a term, "news you can use." While background information about, say, the personality of an air force commander certainly is interesting and can be useful, it is not as valuable as determining how that same commander plans to fight the air battle, the disposition of his forces, or the presence of any new weapons system.

Thanks to the efforts of the CIA, special operations forces, and the Iraqi National Congress, there was no shortage of actionable intelligence and it was of exceptionally high quality, helping the allied forces to keep Saddam Hussein's regime off-balance throughout Operation Iraqi Freedom. In Operation Iraqi Freedom, the integration of military special operations forces and the clandestine services of the Central Intelligence Agency was a marked success. We should build and improve on that success.

Special Operations:

The performance of special operations forces in Iraq confirmed the lesson we had learned in Afghanistan: special operations forces have entered a new era. In the past, most policymakers and high-ranking officers considered special operations forces useful only for such tasks as reconnaissance, raiding, surveillance, and hostage rescue. Their high profile and relatively lavish financial resources made them objects of resentment by many in the military who often derided them as "snake eaters" whose machismo (and financial resources) was in inverse proportion to their usefulness on the battlefield.

Improvements in technology related to communications and targeting gave special operations forces the ability to work closely with U.S. air power, using precision munitions, at the tactical and strategic level. In turn, that "marriage" of technology, highly trained personnel, and firepower gives these forces a striking power and presence on the battlefield that is hugely disproportionate to their numbers.

This does not mean that the special operations forces have abandoned their more traditional roles. Leapfrogging out of Kurdish-held areas in Iraq and bases in Kuwait and Jordan, coalition special operations forces established bases in western Iraq (bases that were known as H-1, H-2, and H-3) and from there went on to deploy via special operations helicopters and transport aircraft like MH-47s, MH-53s, and MC-130s, to conduct raiding and reconnaissance missions. Special operations forces seized the Iraqi oil fields, preserving them from sabotage, as well as many of the river crossings that were vital to the rapid coalition advance toward Baghdad.

Based on their performance in Afghanistan and Iraq, Secretary Rumsfeld's commitment to improving and expanding U.S. special operations capabilities is absolutely justified. Any military spending that sharpens the sword, rather than extending the tail of noncombat forces, is money well spent.

Above It All—Coalition Airpower:

The story of airpower in Operation Iraqi Freedom can be summed up in two words—*precision* and *lethality*. We remember how awestruck some reporters were about the use of precision weapons by U.S. warplanes in the 1991 Gulf War. Often lost in the gee-whiz journalism about cruise missiles and laser-guided bombs was the fact that only about 13 percent of the aerial bombs used in that war were precision-guided weapons. In Operation Iraqi Freedom, almost 70 percent of all munitions used by U.S. airpower were precision-guided weapons, a five-fold increase. Moreover, all strike aircraft in the U.S. inventory—to include the B-1s, B-2s, and B-52s of the U.S. heavy-bomber force—now are capable of using these precision munitions. Considering the bomb loads of an aircraft like a B-2, *one aircraft* can engage *multiple targets* with a reasonable assurance of destroying them. Under the old airpower paradigm (even during the Gulf War), *multiple aircraft* had to engage a *single target* to ensure its destruction.

Advances in intelligence, surveillance, and reconnaissance (ISR) technologies are what give precision munitions actionable targets. Spaced-based systems such as reconnaissance satellites and aerial systems such as JSTARS (Joint Surveillance Target Attack Radar System) and unmanned aerial vehicles (UAVs), such as Global Hawk and the Predator, give commanders the ability to get a clearer picture of the battlefield and detect and monitor the movements of enemy forces. If special operations forces conduct intelligence, reconnaissance, and surveillance, they can send the information they gather via satellite communications systems that are virtually undetectable and that cannot be jammed.

Many of the U.S. aircraft that participated in Operation Iraqi Freedom were fighters (like the Navy and Marine Corps F/A-18s, U.S. Air Force F-16s). They flew into action from U.S. aircraft carriers, including some in the Mediterranean Sea, as well as from bases in Qatar, Kuwait, and Turkey. These attack aircraft needed aerial refueling to operate in theater and did not have extended "loiter time" over the battlefield. The targeting information provided by the improved ISR assets meant that these aircraft could be directed to targets almost immediately. Thus, each sortie usually ended in a successful attack on enemy forces.

JSTARS gave battlefield commanders the information they needed to fight the "deep battle," that is to strike Iraqi units as they moved toward U.S. ground forces. Coalition commanders created what were essentially "no-move zones" in which any vehicle on the road was considered a viable target and subjected to air attacks. If a large enough formation was detected, its area of operations was designated a "killbox" and vast amounts of firepower were brought to bear upon those units. In a few instances, in an attempt to avoid detection, Iraqi commanders ordered their men to abandon their vehicles and attack the U.S. forces on foot, a decision that led to horrific Iraqi casualties and a faster Allied advance toward Baghdad.

The precision of the coalition air effort meant that even in Baghdad and other cities, hitting crucial military and regime facilities did not require that entire neighborhoods be drenched in high explosives. Baghdad and other cities were not pulverized, huge numbers of Iraqis were not killed and injured, and there was no mass exodus of Iraqis from the cities. The huge humanitarian crisis that many critics said would result from the war never materialized.

The Iraqi strategy was, apparently, a defense-in-depth of Baghdad, the epicenter of the Ba'athist regime, shielded by remnants of the Republican Guard, the Special Republican Guard, the irregulars of the Saddam fedayeen (and the Ba'athist militias that they forced onto the battlefield), and the foreign jihadists. They threw themselves at the mechanized juggernauts of the 3rd Infantry Division and the 1st Marine Division, and were defeated in turn.

To his enormous credit, Air Force Lt. General Buzz Mosley, who was the Combined Forces Air Component Commander, took a risk and ordered U.S. aircraft to ignore worries about supposed Baghdad air defenses and offered full air support as U.S. ground forces moved into Baghdad. As U.S. ground forces made their "thunder runs" into Baghdad and later took up their positions within the city—including the international airport—they benefited from the close air support of aircraft like the A-10, an aircraft purpose-built for close air support and ground attack. These aircraft could participate so effectively in the attacks because of U.S. tactical "urban close air support" methods, in which various aircraft of differing size and equipped with differing armament are held in orbit, ready to come to the support of ground forces or hit targets of opportunity. It was a B-1 bomber flying an urban close air support mission that came within an ace of hitting Saddam Hussein as he took cover in a bunker under a Baghdad restaurant (fearful for his own security and suspicious of people around him, he left the structure after only a few minutes).

The 360-Degree Battlefield:

Updating the visual displays that showed the advance of U.S. and coalition forces into Iraq was part of our job as analysts on FOX News Channel. One bit of pioneer reporting we were able to do was to purchase commercial satellite imagery that allowed our viewers to see the battlefield as though they were flying in an airplane. That broadened the view a bit because most reporters—including the embedded reporters who did such terrific work—inevitably see the battlefield through a "straw." That image of the straw was given to us by Oliver North, who mentioned to us that that was how it struck him as an embedded reporter: reporters saw the battlefield through their own inescapably narrow view of it. Our satellite imagery could put these embedded reporter snapshots of reality into a larger context. The "Fox Flyovers," as they came to be called, emanated from the Air Force's POWERSCENE system that had been developed by Cambridge Research Associates.

Taking an even bigger view, one could see a truly revolutionary change in American military doctrine unfolding before us on the battlefield. Not long after the advance on Baghdad began, we were plotting on our maps both the Army's deep penetration, spearheaded by the 3rd Infantry Division, and the 1st Marine Division's run toward the Iraqi capital. As we did so, we realized that the advances were not on a broad, common front; instead, they were like the thrusts of two spears. Moreover, the "spear thrusts" were not operating in what some former military men would recognize as the standard mode—a two brigade- or regiment-front with a brigade or regiment held in reserve. They were moving toward their objectives as separate, apparently self-supporting units, exchanging information with each other by satellite communications. They did so with no diminution of combat power, and the results were impressive.

In the battlefield of the future, there will be no division between the forward echelon and the rear echelon. In any direction a soldier looks, there will be the "front line." This will demand new, imaginative methods for keeping units supplied—the Marines used KC-130 aircraft, landing on hastily modified highways, to do the job—and a recognition that every deployed unit is essentially a combat unit and needs to be combat-ready.

Another lesson from Operation Iraqi Freedom is that the Army and Marines no longer need to fight in the familiar "package" of the division. During the campaign, the Marines created various scratch task forces out of different units—light armored reconnaissance battalions, infantry companies—and sent them off on limited assignments. This model worked well and there is no reasonable obstacle to the creation of these types of task-oriented units on a larger scale.

Size Does Not Matter:

Since the 1980s, the U.S. military has held that it must—and will—come at any enemy with overwhelming force. Enduring conventional wisdom defines as a requirement that the U.S. forces come to the battlefield with roughly the same number of troops as the enemy, in other words, a numerical quota. The results of Operation Iraqi Freedom, however, will demand a redefinition of "overwhelming force" that looks less at numbers of troops and more at sheer firepower. In many battlefields of the future, a smaller force—well equipped, well armed, and well trained—that can move to its objectives swiftly, avoid obstacles nimbly, and deliver accurate, overwhelming firepower, will be considered an overwhelming force.

Close the Door:

As in Operation Enduring Freedom, there was a flaw in the execution of Operation Iraqi Freedom. In the fight for Tora Bora in Afghanistan, our forces effectively and impressively drove the enemy before them. There was, however, no blocking force toward which to drive, an anvil upon which the enemy could be hammered. In Operation Iraqi Freedom, the coalition left the "back door" open, specifically, the Baghdad-to-Damascus road. Over that route, jihadists were able to enter Iraq and members of Saddam Hussein's regime and, according to our sources, weapons of mass destruction and their components were able to leave the country.

"DID THE WAR IN IRAQ MAKE THE WORLD, MAKE THE UNITED STATES, SAFER?"

The answer is certainly, resoundingly, yes. Here are some benefits that we think Operation Iraqi Freedom brought to the world at large:

An End to Aggression:

The danger of Saddam Hussein's pursuit of a Greater Iraq, a threat especially to the Gulf States, is over. Also over is Iraq's thumbing its nose at UN resolutions and the Desert Storm cease-fire agreements—violations that seriously undercut the West's credibility with rogue states. These acts of "diplomatic aggression" have been punished and other states put on notice.

Iraqi WMD:

After he resigned his position, David Kay, who was in charge of the post-liberation effort to find Iraqi WMD, said that while he found no weapons per se there was ample evidence of attempts to reconstitute weapons programs and, amid reports of widespread corruption, there are abundant and well-founded suspicions that people involved in the Iraqi WMD program sold weapons and technical know-how to anybody with enough money—including terrorists. David Kay's overall assessment was that Iraq was more dangerous than we had initially envisioned. Though we are now supposed to believe that every intelligence agency in the world was wrong in its assessment that Iraq had weapons of mass destruction, we agree with Secretary Donald Rumsfeld that it is much more likely that these weapons will eventually be found; indeed, we believe that some intelligence agencies already know where they are.

Syria:

Faced with countries friendly to the United States on three fronts and with his back to the Mediterranean Sea that could bring the United States Navy and Marine Corps to his doorstep, the president of Syria, Bashar Assad, admitted to possessing weapons of mass destruction (chemical weapons), although he said he is unwilling to give them up until Israel disposes of its nuclear weapons. Syria has even begun to talk peace with Israel, albeit very, very quietly. Syria punches above its weight when it comes to terrorism only because its support of terrorism goes essentially unchallenged. We are now in a position to effectively challenge it.

Libya:

Libya's longtime dictator Muammar Gaddafi has recently taken steps to try to reconcile with the West, especially by renouncing his pursuit of weapons of mass destruction, and allowing international inspectors into Libya to verify that his programs are being dismantled. His WMD program was apparently far more advanced than intelligence agencies had previously assumed. In addition, a delegation from Libya has traveled to Israel, with the purpose of talking peace—and even, perhaps, diplomatic recognition of the Jewish state. We know that Gaddafi was inspired to make these steps by watching Saddam Hussein's fall.

Israel:

With the demise of Iraq's Ba'athist regime, Israel no longer has to fear a land invasion, but must fear Iran's nuclear development. This is now Israel's most important national security concern.

Iran:

Although there are indications that the Iranian nuclear program remains active and the internal political crisis in Iran is heightening, the regime in Tehran told representatives of the United Kingdom, France, and Germany that it would allow inspectors from the International Atomic Energy Administration to visit its nuclear facilities. However, they have failed to do so. In addition, the IAEA revealed that Iran has failed to disclose its possession of plans for an advanced uranium centrifuge machine and the diagrams drawn up by Pakistan, only after they were found in Libya. IAEA officials believe that Iran is probably still hiding its own copy of an atomic bomb design supplied by the Pakistani network to Libya. Furthermore, they are still assembling centrifuges, and foreign minister Kamal Kharrazi announced that Iran intends to begin exporting nuclear fuel. While Europe continues to procrastinate diplomatically, the time is fast approaching for a coalition of the willing to take action or let Israel do it. This incessant deception and lying will only continue until the regime is changed.

Pakistan:

Despite the political risk of infuriating the strong Islamist political parties in his country, Pakistan's president Pervez Musharraf has worked hard to cooperate in the war on terror and pulled the curtain back on the corruption and secret deals of those involved with Pakistan's nuclear program, the most prominent of which was the "Father of Pakistan's Bomb," A. Q. Khan. Pakistani investigators have concluded that two senior nuclear scientists—Khan and Mohammed Farooq—used a network of middlemen operating on the black market to supply nuclear weapons technology to Iran, North Korea, and Libya for which they received millions of dollars. This further reinforces the theory of the Web of Terror and the danger these nations pose through their development of WMD and their provision of them to terrorists.

Only if the governments themselves change will we be able to defeat al-Qaeda and other terrorist groups.

President Musharraf has also met with Turkish officials to work out the terms of an agreement to counter the spread of radical Islam. And President Musharraf has announced that Pakistan and India will begin talks at resolving the country's conflicts over Kashmir (where Islamist terrorists are also active and supported by many in Pakistan). Our invasion of Iraq has given Musharraf courage to go after the Islamist threat in his own country.

The United States:

Finally we need to remember what Operation Iraqi Freedom showed to the world. It showed Iraqis greeting U.S. troops, it exposed Saddam for the mass murderer that he was, and it will soon demonstrate how we have helped give birth to an Iraqi democracy that could be a model for the region. Equally important, it should remind hostile, terror-sponsoring dictators of another important lesson: don't mess with the U.S.

CHAPTER SIX

SHARPENING THE SWORD: MILITARY TRANSFORMATIONS

THE APPARENT EASE WITH WHICH the U.S. military and its allies scored impressive victories in Afghanistan and Iraq surprised many people across the world as well as in Congress, the news media, and the Muslim states—but it didn't surprise us.

The dire predictions that the U.S. military would suffer the same fate as the Soviet army in Afghanistan (bogged down in a decade-long war) and the Russian army in Chechnya (smashing cities with artillery and aerial bombardment) did not come to pass—and never would have. Now some of these misguided observers say that our victories in Iraq and Afghanistan were so swift only because our enemies were so inept. They're still wrong.

There are many reasons for why the campaigns went so well, among them: our undeniable technological edge, the superior training of our troops (including training in joint operations), and our outstanding logistical capabilities. Our coalition partners—for example, Great Britain and Australia—have provided superbly trained forces and we have received extremely important contributions—in the form of "boots on the ground," ships at sea, and diplomatic support—from other nations (e.g., Canada).

The seamlessness of our joint operations is the explanation for our successes that many outside, nonmilitary observers are most likely to miss. General Tommy Franks learned a lot about joint operations in Afghanistan with Operation Enduring Freedom and he put that knowledge to extremely good use in Operation Iraqi Freedom. His "education" was accelerated thanks to Defense Secretary Donald Rumsfeld, whose ideas about transforming our military are exactly right. Their implementation of Secretary Rumsfeld's ideas needs to be accelerated because, no matter how impressive our battlefield successes in Afghanistan and Iraq, if we are to destroy the Web of Terror, we need to do much more to improve our war-fighting capabilities.

The modern battlefield has changed dramatically. And while we are current masters of the art, we are not doing enough to reshape our military to retain our advantages. The five dimensions of modern warfare—air, land, sea, space, and information—can be, and must be, far better integrated to defeat our enemies. The goal is not only speed of execution, as demonstrated in the Afghan and Iraq campaigns, but also the disruption of the enemy's "decision cycle" so that his command-and-control apparatus completely breaks down. If that happens, an enemy army and the regime above it can be routed with a minimum of casualties. It is a form of warfare often described as "effects-based." Physical destruction of an enemy army is not the goal of combat operation; casting it into utter disarray, however, is.

HOW WE FIGHT: BLITZ WARFARE

"Blitz warfare"—not to be confused with blitzkrieg—puts a premium on quickly deployable and extremely mobile forces acting in concert. In past wars, the normal doctrine was sequential operations, conducted by individual services. So there was the "softening-up" phase conducted by Army artillery or Air Force air strikes that "prepared" a battlefield prior to the attack, then an attack phase led by ground units of the Army or Marine Corps, followed by a consolidation phase. Blitz warfare demands simultaneous operations that dramatically compress the phases of warfare. In turn, this demands *precision*, precision of military integration and precision of targeting, which is why it is so vital that the American military ensures it has matchless information and precision guidance technologies. Today, we can pinpoint crucial targets to a degree previously unimaginable, and because we can, we can minimize civilian casualties; indeed, we can limit them to what amount to deadly accidents. Remember that while the government sector of Baghdad was subjected to intense bombardment, most of the city was left untouched. We were able to strike government buildings and other enemy targets even when they were in civilian neighborhoods.

Blitz warfare is *networked* warfare. Communications technology now allows the president of the United States to speak simultaneously with a regional commander, the commander of an armored brigade, and the captain of a warship—all of whom may be many hundreds of miles from one another. It provides the battlefield commanders with the ability to speak, exchange data, and share images with subordinates and vice versa. Battle is chaos, but this networking allows information gathered by sensors on and above the battlefield to reach those who most need it, giving them "situational awareness" of the battlefield and the areas around it. As an example, the Global Hawk unmanned aerial vehicle has a capability called Advanced Information Architecture which enables ground forces to bring the information from the Global Hawk's sensors (infrared, television, and radar) directly to a personal display accessory as small as an iPAQ or Palm Pilot *within eleven seconds.* This is like giving a company commander almost instant access to a reconnaissance satellite. While this breaks the usual intelligence chain of dissemination, it enables our forces to move faster, so fast that an enemy can't react effectively. That's how we get inside the enemy's decision cycle, and so ensure that he's trying to react to our first move while we've already committed our second move. During Operation Iraqi Freedom, we had great success integrating information from sensor systems like the aircraft-borne Joint Surveillance and Target Attack Radar System (JSTARS); unmanned systems like Global Hawk, Predator, and satellites; human and signal intelligence; and the Blue Force Tracker that uses digital "ID tags" on each vehicle and satellite communications in order to help ground forces locate other friendly units. Together, these information sources gave commanders an unparalleled view of the battlefield and targeting information. And that allowed commanders to bring overwhelming firepower almost anywhere on the battlefield with speed and accuracy.

Other information warfare efforts—involving coalition intelligence, the Iraqi National Congress, and those Iraqis brave enough to aid the anti-Ba'athist cause—helped convince many Iraqi soldiers and their commanders that the right decision for them was to simply fade away from the battle.

Our development of high technology like this has made a dramatic improvement in joint warfare, but these improvements cannot stop. We need to keep pace, because it is blitz warfare that gives America a sharper sword and, thus, greater diplomatic clout, which means saving lives and improving our national security. It is blitz warfare that can liberate North Korea with much less damage and loss of life than many analysts think—and that, even short of war, can bring North Korea to the bargaining table ready to surrender its WMD capability, just as Libya has promised to do.

THE WEAPONS WE NEED

The battlefield of the future will not conform to the U.S. order of battle just because the Pentagon wishes it were so. We cannot think in terms of tinkering with the military structure leftover from the Cold War, adding a little here, taking away a little there. We need a thorough transformation—which is, in fact, one of the stated goals of the Bush administration.

Donald Rumsfeld's business experience, his reputation as a cost-cutter and efficiency specialist, and, most of all, his readiness to embrace high technology, Special Forces units, integrated "actionable" intelligence, joint operations, and innovative military thinking make him the right man for the job. What our military needs is not greater numbers but an effort to "balance the force" so that there is a much higher proportion of war fighters in active, Guard, and Reserve units; so that more of our units are mobile and capable of quick response; and so that we make the utmost use of high technology, because such technology is crucial to making our lean and often out-numbered forces much more lethal than their adversaries.

I   I   I   I   I   I   I   I   I

The first item on the Transformation "To Do" list is to reshape the military in terms of expeditionary forces. During the Cold War, the Navy and the Marine Corps deployed forces on a regular basis to the Pacific, the Mediterranean, and other areas around the world, often in aircraft carrier task forces, later in aircraft carrier battle groups and Marine Amphibious Units, and later, in Marine Expeditionary Units. Today, the Navy and the Marines remain organized for rapid embarkation and deployment. Even though the Marines have heavy equipment and weapons, their largest and "heaviest" units are "medium" at best.

Even more important than the "portability" of Marine Corps and Navy units is their "expeditionary" organizational structure and mindset. The Navy sends aircraft carrier battle groups (CVBGs) around the world and Marines often embark as part of a Marine Expeditionary Unit (MEU)—a reinforced infantry battalion that has its own organic artillery, aviation (a combined helicopter squadron and six Harrier Vertical and/or Short Take-off and Landing, VSTOL, jets), and supply and maintenance units—on board a three-ship Navy amphibious ready group (ARG). The sailors and Marines attached to a CVBG or an ARG-MEU team know they will face a regular schedule of training, "work-ups," deployment, and return. They also have a rough idea of when they will deploy, know where they will be deployed (at least initially), and are mindful that they might be required to perform any number of tasks during their deployment. Marines and sailors accept all that as part of what they do.

Recently, the Navy and the Marine Corps developed a new formation that provides improved capabilities for the MEU-ARG team: the expeditionary strike group (ESG). The basic three-ship ARG and its embarked Marines are "married" to a guided missile cruiser, two other surface combatants (cruisers, destroyers, or frigates), an attack submarine, and a P-3 Orion maritime patrol aircraft. These assets provide greater offensive strength in the form of the ships' cruise missiles and guns and better defensive capabilities as well. The current Chief of Naval Operations, Admiral Vern Clark, has introduced the concept of "surge operations" with his CVBGs, which allows the Navy to rapidly bring six carriers to a theater of operations (as was done in Operation Iraqi Freedom).

The U.S. Air Force has embraced the expeditionary concept as well, albeit in a different mode from that of the Navy and the Marine Corps. The demands placed on the Air Force by Operation Northern Watch and Operation Southern Watch—the enforcement of no-fly zones over northern and southern Iraq—overstretched the service and prompted justifiable complaints from pilots and other personnel about the strains on personnel and machines. So the Air Force reformulated the entire service as an "expeditionary air and space force" capable of fielding ten "air and space expeditionary forces." Essentially, these ten "AEFs" are all of roughly equal combat power and draw personnel and equipment from all over the Air Force for possible deployment. Moreover, almost every uniformed member of the Air Force—officer and enlisted alike—knows he or she is liable for service with an AEF on a deployment of up to fifteen months. As with the Navy and Marine Corps, this certain knowledge of expected duty makes for better morale.

The Air Force is used to operating out of bases with extensive infrastructure. In the new warfare, such bases won't always be available. The campaign in Afghanistan brought home to the Air Force the need to establish and operate new bases in forward areas, and to be able to do so at short notice. The Air Force got the message. Between February 2003 and April 2003, the Air Force established a dozen bases in the Persian Gulf region, including five established in Iraq during Operation Iraqi Freedom.

Until Afghanistan and Iraq, the heavy units of the Army had not had much recent expeditionary warfare experience, stationed as they long had been in Europe during the Cold War and in South Korea, where their mission was (or is) to stop massive ground offensives. The Army has had, however, ample experience in peacekeeping operations, sending units to Bosnia, the Sinai Peninsula, and elsewhere.

Still, it is telling that the Army's initial reaction to Special Forces successes in Afghanistan was to follow up by deploying a heavy, mechanized force. The Army still thinks in terms of the Cold War conventional operations it has long trained for, relying on a long logistical tail and a large base structure in the United States and Europe. But that won't do for the War on Terror. Thankfully, the Army's new chief of staff, General Peter Schoomaker, whose background is in special operations and light infantry, is attempting to rework the Army's approach to expeditionary warfare and make its units more able to participate in joint expeditionary operations. We strongly endorse the secretary of defense's initiative in selecting General Schoomaker and the initiatives he is starting toward the transformation of the Army at this time. But it is just a beginning, with much to do.

If the first need is for the military to think in terms of expeditionary units, the second is to consider how to wring more combat power out of our force structure. Many in Congress want to expand the armed forces—particularly the Army. It is true that our military is overstretched, and that our National Guard and Reserve forces are overburdened. But we believe that this is not because our military force structure is too small, but because it has been given tasks beyond the waging of war. Secretary Rumsfeld already has identified approximately 245,000 jobs across the Department of Defense that could be outsourced to contractors. Our recommendation: outsource the jobs, use the savings to improve the lot of the "trigger pullers," and create new frontline fighting units while phasing out paper-pushing ones. In other words, change the "tail to tooth" ratio so there is less tail and more teeth.

Personnel are the highest priced item in the Department of Defense budget, so rather than reflexively expand the number of billets, the Pentagon should make better and more efficient use of the current personnel levels. The Army should follow the lead of the Air Force, which within its Air and Space Expeditionary Forces makes every member of, say, the Air Staff in the Pentagon liable for deployment. The advantage of this is that it trims the support tail of the force and eliminates occupational redundancy. For example, doctors, nurses, and medics who are stationed at the Walter Reed Army Hospital or the Brooks Army Medical Center should be part of an "expeditionary medical unit" that could be deployed as an "expeditionary support element." *Every* member of the armed forces should be combat zone deployable. If they aren't, their function should be outsourced, or eliminated.

Another way to get greater combat power out of the current force structure is to change the way the Army and Marine Corps are structured for combat. First, the Army needs to get "lighter"—that is to say, have smaller and less layered headquarters and fewer armored, mechanized infantry, field artillery, and air defense artillery units in its inventory. That means that the Army might not need as many tanks as it currently has in its inventory or as many self-propelled artillery pieces. Heavy forces are still needed and vitally important, but lighter units in expeditionary forces should be the priority, because they are more likely to see combat against the threats we face now. And as part of that restructuring the Army will need to enlarge its Special Forces and focus to a greater degree on unconventional warfare and integrating with the CIA. The Army must get away from the notion of fighting in division-sized elements (and larger) and think more in terms of fighting brigades or combat groups that have a mix of light, medium, and heavy forces. Taking a cue from the Marine Corps, the Army must ensure that any Army unit operating in the joint expeditionary warfare environment will be capable of independent operations and possessed of adequate air and ground mobility, firepower, and combat service support.

This isn't a new idea. In World War II, the U.S. Army's armored divisions in northwestern Europe adopted an organization that divided their striking forces into two combined-arms teams of roughly equivalent structures known as "combat commands." In World War II and Korea, the Army also developed units known as "regimental combat teams." In both instances, these formations were configured for independent combat operations. Even today the Army has Separate Infantry Brigades (like the 173rd Airborne Brigade which secured the northern front area of Iraq) that are very capable units.

What the Army needs are deployable "brigade combat groups," of five thousand troops—including light infantry, airborne or air assault forces, and/or armor/mechanized units/artillery with a support brigade integrated into joint expeditionary forces. For soldiers, the notion of fixed deployments must be as familiar as it is for sailors and Marines. A set deployment schedule not only improves joint operations combat training but also is more conducive to family stability, morale, and personnel retention than are the seemingly endless deployments of a few unfortunate units. Also as an aid to morale and performance, units—not individual soldiers rotating in and out—should be sent on deployments.

As of this printing, the Army, by 2007, expects to have created a modular army by divesting Cold War headquarters and structures, moving to brigade-based organizations from today's division-based formations, and restructuring the reserve components. We strongly endorse the Army's initiative in this area.

In addition, we need a new and modern mobilization program for the Guard and Reserve, not the antiquated system left over from the

Cold War. Guard and Reserve troops are no longer "weekend warriors." Their contributions to the war on terror have been invaluable; indeed, if it were not for the service of these citizen-soldiers—so often characterized by experience and maturity—our forces would have been severely hamstrung in the campaigns we have conducted since September 2001.

If the regular forces are reconfigured as expeditionary forces, it makes sense for many "heavy" armor and artillery units to become the province of the National Guard and Reserve. Moreover, given the nature of the war on terror, other units well represented in the reserves—military police and intelligence units—would be better placed in the regular forces.

Another related issue confronting the U.S. military is what to do with its Cold War basing structure. Even after widespread base closings in the 1990s, many military facilities in the United States are of dubious value. In general, as far as domestic basing is concerned, the chief question policymakers need to ask is whether the deployable units at the base are within quick reach of proper transport facilities. If not, the base should be closed and the units moved to another base.

Overseas—and in Europe especially—if you looked at a map of American bases you might think that the Cold War was still on. In the Pacific theater, because of the North Korean threat, we still need our deployments in Japan and we are already restructuring our system of bases in South Korea. Many European bases—with a few significant exceptions, like Ramstein Air Base in Germany—can be closed, since Europe is no longer a likely battlefield for the United States.

Much more important is to have a chain of forward operating bases ("lily pads") in Central Asia, South Asia, and the Middle East. Because the units stationed on them would be rotating through on a fixed deployment cycle or using them for sustained combat operations, there would be no need to develop dependent housing and other infrastructure that makes many of the old Cold War bases so expensive.

Money saved by closing unnecessary bases should go into modernizing our military hardware. Currently all the services are facing block obsolescence. Some vehicles are approaching fifty years in age, many of our airborne tankers are more than forty years old, and even a large number of Air Force fighter aircraft have been in service for more than two decades. To recapitalize its current force structure, the Department of Defense needs to spend about $118 billion annually; instead, it is spending around $73 billion plus a year. Combat and support operations in the war on terror are consuming most, if not all, of the increases in the defense budget. Because our forces now operate at a much higher operational tempo—with dramatic increases in combat operations—and because during the Clinton administration modernization spending averaged around $50 billion per year, the Department of Defense has a $400 billion shortfall in modernization expenditures.

One way to overcome this hurdle is with smaller units using new and more effective technologies. For example, using the unmanned Global Hawk in place of Navy P-3s for broad-area maritime surveillance and in place of U-2s for surveillance and reconnaissance would enable Defense to save at least one billion dollars per year.

Another good example is the cancellation of the advanced helicopter program called Comanche that was terminated in late February 2004. The resources for these aircraft should be reallocated to restructure and revitalize Army aviation to meet current and future needs.

Changes like these can significantly reduce our replacement costs but we need to look at other savings too. Getting the most bang for the buck isn't just a cliché, it's the way military planners and congressional budget-setters have to think. And if done properly, as we've outlined here, it can actually sharpen our nation's sword to an even keener edge.

CHAPTER SEVEN

BURNISHING THE SHIELD

I N THE GOLDEN AGE OF THE GREEK city-states, when the likes of Athens and Sparta were at the zenith of their power and glory, the dominant force on the battlefields of ancient Greece was the heavy infantryman, the hoplite. The hoplite's weapons were valuable to him because they were what he used to strike at his enemies; likewise his helmet because it protected his head and face from missiles and blows. The bronze shield, however, had an almost mystical importance to these citizen-soldiers. It was an important personal possession; it often was inherited, and a hoplite's mother or wife placed good-luck totems inside the shield's bowl. Legend has it that Spartan wives and mothers sternly reminded their sons and husbands of their duty to Sparta by telling the men to come home with their shields or on them. A hoplite considered the loss of his shield to be a great disgrace.

On the battlefield, the shield did not protect its owner per se but the man to his left; therefore, every soldier in formation depended on the man next to him. This relationship of trust and mutual defense in an infantry formation became a metaphor for the hoplites and their relationship with the city-states. If the hoplites failed, they were guilty of letting their larger shield slip, and thus endangering the city-state.

To the enemy, advancing hoplites appeared as a wall of shields. Above those shields was a forest of spears that, at a given signal, came down, pointing toward the enemy. In order to instill discipline and pride in their men as well as to lend their advancing formation an even more fearsome aspect, commanders often would order their men to burnish their shields to a bright shine before battle.

We've spoken of the need to transform the U.S. military. If you will, that was sharpening the sword. Now, we want to discuss how to burnish the shield.

TIME FOR A NEW ALLIANCE

In times of war, any nation automatically looks for allies. In World War I, the British and the French desperately hoped that the Americans would arrive in time to turn the tide against the Kaiser and actively worked to accelerate U.S. entrance into that conflict. In June 1941, Winston Churchill swallowed his decades-long hatred of Soviet Communism and gladly welcomed the Soviet Union into the war against the Nazis. In the late 1940s, the United States led the effort to create alliances that would act as bulwarks against the Soviet Union and successfully created not only NATO, but also the Central Treaty Organization (CENTO) and the Southeast Asia Treaty Organization (SEATO).

In the War on Terror, the United States never has gone it alone—and never will. Soon after the attacks of September 11, 2001, NATO affirmed its founding principle that an attack on one is an attack on all, and NATO played (and still plays) an important role in Afghanistan. Although some of the countries that had participated in the Afghan campaign refused to participate in the liberation of Iraq, the United States still has been able to count on the assistance of such countries as Britain, Australia, Japan, South Korea, the Philippines, Thailand, Italy, Spain, Poland, Denmark, Hungary, Bulgaria, Ukraine, Romania, the Netherlands, Norway, El Salvador, and nearly twenty other countries.

The "coalition of the willing" doesn't exist as an institution but as an active reality. Another example of such an informal institution is the U.S.-led Proliferation Security Initiative (PSI). When Libya agreed to give up its nuclear weapons program after Operation Iraqi Freedom, it did so *not* because of the diplomatic efforts of the UN or NATO, but because of British and American diplomatic efforts coordinated through the instrument of the PSI. The PSI is committed to preventing the proliferation of WMDs and to do so by the interdiction of WMD weapons, delivery systems, components, and materials. The PSI has no formal organization; as one administration official told the *Wall Street Journal*, it is "an activity, not an organization." This loose group of nations dedicated to counter-proliferation is centered on sixteen countries—Australia, Canada, Denmark, the Netherlands, the United Kingdom, Poland, France, Portugal, Germany, Spain, Italy, Singapore, Turkey, Japan, Norway, and the United States—but as many as fifty nations have stated that they agree with the PSI's principles and will lend aid whenever they are needed.

The fact that the PSI is an "activity," not an organization, means that it is dedicated to action, not bureaucracy. And the cliché is true: Actions speak louder than words. In September 2003, a freighter, bound for Libya and carrying parts used in the machinery used to enrich uranium, was diverted to an Italian port. There, police and customs officials searched the ship and seized its cargo. In August 2003, at the request of the United States, port officials in Taiwan boarded a freighter headed to North Korea and confiscated its cargo— ingredients for chemical weapons. These cooperative actions between states committed to preventing weapons proliferation are all that is needed to get the job done. What the war on terror does not need is a formal alliance or organization that risks creating *another* bureaucracy to support it.

At most, what would be useful is a *short* document—no more than one page—called "The Freedom from Terrorism Charter," laying out our commitment to destroy the regimes that make up the Web of Terror and foster the creation of free and open societies in their place. Countries that are demonstrably committed to democratic values and to defeating the Web of Terror can sign it as a statement of common principles. As an informal alliance, it would be flexible to varying strategic needs, and provide a global answer to the question of why we fight.

Along with the sixteen participants in the PSI, we should solicit a signature from India—first, because it is the world's largest democracy; second, because it is geo-strategically pivotal; third, because it is economically and technologically advanced; fourth, because it has a large and capable military (with substantial combat experience) and a first-rate intelligence service. And it is a natural ally against radical Islam.

For those who are keen on creating another formal alliance, we would ask them: "What treaty bound the Grand Alliance of World War II—the United States, the United Kingdom, and the Soviet Union—from December 1941 to September 1945?" Common interests are what make an alliance real, not vast bureaucracies churning out masses of paperwork.

REFORMING AMERICAN DIPLOMACY

The State Department often does unheralded, hard, and brilliant work. But America's diplomatic culture, which in our experience is found mostly *outside* the actual State Department—in Congress, the administration, think tanks, academia, and the news media—is in obvious need of reform. This culture values "process" (like a "peace process") no matter how negligible the results. It values "engagement" with hostile countries even if engagement gets us nothing. It values diplomatic courtesy to hostile countries even if such courtesy disheartens and undercuts democratic opposition groups that are our natural friends and allies.

The president needs to make it clear to the practitioners and advocates of "soft" diplomacy that we are in a war. To underline the point with action, the president and the secretary of state need to tell American diplomats that, in almost every mission, they are engaged in political warfare. American diplomats are not sent abroad merely to "observe and report"—although that is part of the job—but to aggressively advance American policy. And the president and secretary of state should make it a priority to appoint and to fire administration officials according to their ability to absorb and enact that message.

America's diplomats cannot be afraid to speak frank truths to the countries to which they are assigned, to ensure that American aid serves American interests (and not line foreign bureaucrats' pockets), and to make America's case for freedom to the country at large, using the local media. We cannot have diplomats hiding in bunkers or practicing quiet diplomacy alone. In this war, they must be public figures, taking risks like our service men and women, because like them, they are on the front line of a war.

In November 2002, Norman Pattiz, chairman of Westwood One and a member of the U.S. Broadcasting Board of Governors, said, "In terms of the Middle East, there is a media war going on. The weapons of that war are hate radio, disinformation, incitement to violence, government censorship, and journalistic self-censorship." Like the Cold War, the war on terror is very much a war of ideas; therefore, it is imperative that the U.S. government strengthen its public diplomacy effort. To its credit, the United States has not shied away from this particular battlefield, establishing one station aimed at Iran, Radio Azadi ("Freedom"), in 1998, and one aimed at the broader region, Radio Sawa ("Together"), in July 2002, under the auspices of the U.S. Broadcasting Board of Governors, which is responsible for such services as Radio Liberty, Radio Free Asia, and the Voice of America.

The story of Radio Azadi—renamed Radio Farda ("Tomorrow") in December 2002—is instructive. The service began broadcasting to Iran in 1998, albeit a mere thirty minutes a day. Predictably, the mullahs of Iran decried it as a "CIA plot" and banned Iranians from making any contact with the service. The people of Iran do not lack for broadcast choices; therefore, many in and out of Iran were skeptical about Radio Azadi's ability to attract and retain an audience. Radio Azadi had prepared well, however—recruiting journalists with experience in Iran, installing an Iranian editor and an energetic staff of young producers and broadcasters in studios in Prague, and adhering to a neutral tone in its newscasts. It soon carved out a niche in the Iran "market" and expanded its program offerings and its broadcast day. Over time, more Iranian academics, artists, students, and intellectuals—inside and outside Iran—began appearing on the show, and consequently Radio Azadi's credibility and audience grew steadily.

Radio Sawa has had its growing pains. Aimed at young people (age fifteen to thirty), its popular music programming gained it a wide audience. However, some in and out of the region have criticized it for insufficient substance and for having insufficient gravity. Whether or not that criticism is fair, Radio Sawa is well worth the effort, since the alternative—allowing state-controlled media and the likes of al-Jazeera a free hand to spin lies about the United States and its policies—is unacceptable.

FIVE FREEDOMS

Military solutions are necessary to some of the strategic challenges we face, but we cannot defeat the Web of Terror solely by military means. We must broadcast to the people of these countries a message of liberation and hope, of freedom and opportunity, of a better life that lies not in terrorism and war but in free markets and democratic governments that respect all peoples and all faiths. Diplomacy with the regimes in question has both its uses and its limits. As we've pointed out, it is in Saudi Arabia's and Pakistan's best interests, for example, to reform their education systems so that their people are taught viable job skills, not inflexible, hate-filled ideology.

But we need to speak directly to the people as well. The infamous al-Jazeera, dozens of state-run radio and television channels, and hundreds of newspapers and magazines in the Islamic world preach against the West and inculcate hatred toward it. We need an effective countervoice. Our popular culture, which strikes many Muslims as poisonous, cannot do the job on its own, and can even be counterproductive. We need a massive infusion of American media, geared to an Islamic audience, that states the case for peace and freedom.

A case in point was the global broadcast of the Super Bowl on February 1, 2004. A great game, but the now notorious half-time show was not only degrading in its own right but also an imbecilic message and image to send out to the world. One might wish that so-called "popular artists" and the corporations that support them might put some semblance of thought into the moral impact—domestic and international—of their product, but they don't. They are, to be blunt, too narrow-minded and stupid to be bothered with that. We need a much more serious approach, one that appeals morally to Muslim men and women, one that shows them the virtues—not just the well-advertised vices—of Western freedom.

For this effort to succeed, the message must speak to the fundamental yearning of every human being for a life that is free from fear and want. We must make the case that democratic governance, an open economy, and a tolerant culture are the best means to fulfill this yearning and to achieve long-lasting peace and prosperity.

Many Islamist websites issue dire warnings about the effects of secular democracy on the moral and social fabric of any Muslim nation so foolish as to adopt it. To answer this argument, we have, thankfully, the example of Turkey; and if we succeed in Iraq, we will have the example of Iraq. But fundamentally we need to show that freedom is not a synonym for libertinism and license.

Immediately before World War II, Franklin Roosevelt summed up what the United States was defending in terms of freedoms: Freedom of Speech, Freedom from Fear, Freedom from Want, and Freedom of

Religion, which inspired Norman Rockwell's famous paintings illustrating the freedoms. We suggest that today America needs to internationally broadcast its support for *Five Freedoms*.

Freedom of Education:

In far too many places in the Middle East, the primary mission of the schools is political indoctrination. In Iraq before its liberation, the cult of Saddam Hussein was introduced in primary schools, reinforced through the universities, and then continued for a lifetime through the efforts of the state-run media. In the schools controlled by the Palestinian Authority, Palestinian children are taught to hate Israelis—and Jews in general—from their earliest years. In many of the *madrassas* of Pakistan, where young men are sent to learn the Koran, students receive a radical Islamist political message (most of the Pakistanis who fought for the Taliban were recruited directly from these schools). We should make clear to Muslim parents that freedom of education means giving their children employable skills and hope for a better future, as well as giving parents the opportunity to pass *their* values, rather than the regime's, on to their children.

Freedom of the Economy:

One of the reasons so many states in the Muslim world have failed so miserably is that they have little or no economic freedom. Capitalism is an imperfect system, but it indisputably creates economic prosperity. To flourish, however, it requires freedom and the rule of law.

In many Muslim countries, large industries are controlled by the state, their assets and incomes funneled to members of the ruling party or family and their cronies. In Saudi Arabia, Robert Baer reports in his book *Sleeping with the Devil*, businessmen are constantly worried not about their companies' potential failure but about their potential success. Apparently, some members of the royal family have a habit of forcing successful businessmen to sell their companies to them, usually well below market value. The Palestinian Authority's economic system is one in which people become wealthy because they have close connections with the organization's leadership or have access to the hundreds of millions of dollars in direct foreign aid provided to the Palestinian Authority by many countries. Unfortunately for Palestinians, the only truly successful Palestinian executives are those who live and work in such places as Canada and the United States.

We need to broadcast to the Muslim world that we support private property. That's a message that will resonate. Defining freedom as freedom to own your own land and business independent of state depredations will be popular—and it is necessary for economic and political reform and progress.

Freedom of Information:

When we traveled to Iraq in 2003, one of the most heartening things we encountered was the plethora of publications that had sprung up in the country. We need to do what we can to encourage alternative information outlets. As Iraq's experience shows—and as we know from the Cold War—people living in closed societies yearn for freedom of information.

Freedom of the Person:

In the United States and other Western countries, the freedom to live where we like, to pursue any career, and to participate in a whole range of activities—civic, religious, and charitable—without worry about state approval or interference is taken as a given. But in much of the Muslim world, people are treated as chattels of the ruling party or cabal. Broadcasting to the Islamic world the idea of personal freedom—including freedom from arbitrary arrest—will also resonate.

Freedom of Governance:

Much of the Muslim world brims with frustration and resentment toward rigid, authoritarian governments. We need to show that democratic government will give the people the authority to enact change peacefully through the legislative process and to hold their own elected officials accountable. Getting the Muslim world to focus on democratic domestic politics is the great antidote to what happens now: the projection of radicalized Muslim hatred outward in the form of terrorism. We need to encourage democratization throughout the Muslim world, and to ensure that people have confidence in their electoral system, the United States—or, if necessary, the UN—should be willing to monitor and verify elections, until the efficacy and resilience of democracy has been proved to the people.

There is every chance that freedom and democracy will put down roots in countries like Iraq and even Saudi Arabia. Writing in the *Weekly Standard* in the summer of 2003, the Iranian journalist and author Amir Taheri challenged the idea that there is no Islamic tradition of citizenship. He pointed out that since the tenth and eleventh centuries, there has been a body of Islamic thought that allows for nonauthoritarian governments. At least one Muslim scholar who lived and wrote in the fourteenth century discussed "a secular bond between citizens." One scholar might not impress—except when you stop to consider that many of the Islamist terror groups derive their raison d'être from the writings of a single *thirteenth-century* scholar.

There have been more recent examples of the establishment of democratic institutions—in Morocco, for instance. Even Iran's situation speaks to the potential for a democratic revolution in the region. Were it not for the mullahs' determination to hold on to power and maintain their rigid control over state institutions, including the military and security forces, Iran probably would have a second, more peaceful revolution at the ballot box.

Right now, two Gulf States, Bahrain and Qatar, are democratizing. Since 2001, the ruling family of Bahrain—the al-Khalifas—has been transforming the country from an emirate into a constitutional monarchy. Admittedly, the family still maintains considerable power—the king's uncle is prime minister—but Bahrain has taken the first steps to establish a working democratic state. In Qatar, the monarch, Sheikh

Hamad bin Khalifa al-Thani, has embarked on a broad program of liberalization and gradual reform. A loosening of press restrictions led to
the establishment of al-Jazeera, a mixed blessing to be sure, but al-
Jazeera is not state-controlled and shows other Gulf States that press
freedom need not endanger their governments. The emir's wife plays
a prominent and public role in the country, lending her patronage to
environmental and educational projects. Women in Qatar are allowed
to vote and hold public office.

Morocco is another success story. When King Mohammed VI came
to the throne in 1999, he almost immediately put the country on a
path to constitutional monarchy. In September 2002, Morocco held its
first general election and twenty-six political parties took part. Even
after the Islamist suicide bombings in Casablanca in 2003, Morocco
went ahead with local elections. While the examples of Morocco,
Qatar, and Bahrain might not satisfy some advocates of democracy,
they just might provide examples to the House of Saud that political
reforms do not necessarily mean the end of a dynasty.

The notion that a people cannot "handle" democratic ideas if they
have been yoked to tyranny has diminishing credibility in our information age. Many people in the Middle East have been exposed to
information about democratic government, through either direct experience or the ever more popular means of satellite TV and the Inter-
net. The education level in these countries often is relatively high, and
often there is a substantial middle class who could make the transi-
tion from authoritarian government to democratic government a relatively smooth one. As to the reaction of ordinary people to democracy,
there are many examples of individuals emerging from under authoritarian rule and enthusiastically embracing democracy. Indeed, one of
the more striking images of the 1990s was of the long lines at the polls
in South Africa when that country first held truly free and open elections. People who had never voted before, whose direct experience
with government probably had been with security police enforcing
apartheid, stood for hours in order to cast their votes.

Those who warn us that "culture" will prevent people in the Middle East from embracing the Five Freedoms disregard the example of immigrants from the Middle East, North Africa, and southern Asia to Western Europe, the United States, and Canada—immigrants who have taken quickly to Western freedoms and democratic institutions, and prospered in market economies. We will have succeeded in defeating the Web of Terror when the freedom and success that Muslim immigrants find in the West can be replicated in the countries from which they came.

Another option to encourage that development is the reestablishment of the U.S. Information Agency, which served as America's public relations agency during the Cold War. From 1953 to the late 1990s, when the State Department absorbed it, the USIA managed educational, cultural, and information programs about the United States. A "new" USIA would present to the world those facets of American life that our invasive popular culture does not always show in the best of lights (if it shows them at all). It would explain American perspectives on current events and historical ones, describe how government and politics work in the United States, and show how the Five Freedoms apply in the United States. Based on the security situation in the particular countries, the USIA could reestablish the American cultural centers and libraries that were ubiquitous during the Cold War or extend the "American room" program begun in the 1990s that establishes an area in public libraries dedicated to American literature, history, and culture.

We are mindful of the difficulties involved in breaking through the "static" of state-owned media in the Middle East and countering the effects of decades of propaganda. Based on the many outlandish conspiracy theories we have encountered in the Middle East's official media, our opinion is that it will not be easy getting the new USIA and the new broadcast service accepted as authoritative sources of news and information. Of course, the other side of that statement is that, because of the dubious veracity of state-run and state-controlled news media outlets in the Middle East, millions upon millions of people are hungry for news they can trust.

REMAKING AMERICAN DOMESTIC SECURITY: THE PUBLIC SECURITY ACT OF 2004

Aside from broadcasting our ideas to the Muslim world, we need to do some hard thinking at home too. One of the biggest surprises since September 11, 2001, has been the unwillingness of Congress and the president to reorder fundamentally the U.S. intelligence and domestic security apparatus. In the late 1940s, the United States founded organizations like the National Security Council, the Department of Defense, and the Central Intelligence Agency in part to counter the threat posed by the Soviet Union and to ensure that the United States would not suffer another Pearl Harbor. Yet, apart from the creation of the Department of Homeland Security—which was more a reorganization than a real reform—America's foreign intelligence and domestic security agencies have not been structurally improved. The tiresome turf battles, confounding red tape, and bureaucratic plodding all continue.

The blame for this belongs with Congress, which seems more intent on pork barrel spending as usual than on improving U.S. intelligence and domestic security. The Bush administration bears some blame as well. With the notable exception of the Defense Department, well run under Donald Rumsfeld, it has failed to slash the bureaucracy and improve our security.

Perhaps the welter of controversy over the Patriot Act—a law that we think needs no dramatic revision lest the immense benefits derived from it be lost—and the detention of suspects in Guantánamo Bay, as well as the debate over the Iraqi campaign, diverted the administration from this necessary business. But it remains necessary, and therefore the president needs to introduce a *Public Security Act of 2004* to the Congress immediately.

The act should create a domestic security service devoted to counterterrorism and counterespionage duties, separate from the FBI. The FBI is not a counterterrorism agency but a *law enforcement* agency inhibited by a wide variety of federal laws that hinder counterterrorism work. A new cabinet member would lead the new security service—the U.S. Terrorist Security Department (TSD)—and all terrorism and counterterrorism responsibilities from the FBI and CIA would be moved to the TSD. The TSD would have global reach and responsibilities. It would gather and analyze intelligence and distribute it to the proper local, state, federal, and international authorities. It would conduct surveillance at points of entry to the United States and have the power to arrest and detain suspects. And it would have the authority to launch covert operations against terrorists and their supporters around the world. The goal would be to develop, disseminate, and execute operations based on actionable intelligence as quickly, efficiently, and effectively as possible.

Another necessary reform is the creation of a branch of the federal judiciary known as Special Terrorist Courts, to expedite trials related to terrorism and keep them secure. In these courts, suspects initially classed as "enemy combatants" or criminals abetting terrorism would face a panel of three judges. The judges would both preside over the trials (with prosecuting and defense attorneys) and render the verdicts. There would be no juries (juries pose too many security-related risks) and there would be special rules to protect secret intelligence and counterintelligence information presented as evidence, protect witnesses who might be intelligence or law-enforcement agents or former terrorists, and provide security for judges and prosecutors. Another panel of judges would choose defense attorneys from volunteers who have substantial experience in criminal prosecution at the federal level; these attorneys would be vetted thoroughly and subjected to periodic security checks.

The *Public Security Act of 2004* should detail the special powers that federal authorities can legally exercise, and that can be extended

by Congress as necessary, in order to protect lives and maintain public order in case of a terrorist emergency. Beyond that, as part of the
act, Congress and the president should develop and codify in *law* the
process by which the United States government would reconstitute
itself quickly after a nuclear or other devastating attack on Washington by terrorists.

Laws passed in the mid-1960s concerning the succession to the
presidency make that aspect of our government's survival relatively
clear. The 25th Amendment lays out the process by which the president of the United States can name a vice president if that office
becomes vacant and the vice president can serve as acting president
if the president is incapacitated. The Constitution allows governors to
fill vacant Senate seats by appointment. There is, however, no legal or
constitutional mechanism to fill vacancies in the House of Representatives by appointment in case of a national emergency. To ensure that
the U.S. government can be rebuilt promptly after a strike on the
nation's capital, the Constitution needs to be amended to allow state
governors to fill vacant seats of the U.S. House of Representatives by
appointment, with such appointments limited to members of the same
party as the member who has died or been incapacitated. Similarly,
Congress should enact a law that specifies a sequence of judicial
seniority among federal courts so that automatic appointment can fill
the benches of the Supreme Court in case of a terrorist strike. And
finally, Congress should look to dispersing the various constituent federal departments and agencies that deal with national security.

We shouldn't make ourselves an inviting target. The war on terror
will be conducted not just with the sword. We need the strong shield
that comes with a prudent defense and fallback strategies that plan for
the worst. This preparation, and having workable strategies to deal
with worst-case scenarios, is one of the best ways of preventing them
from happening.

PART THREE

WHY WE FIGHT

CHAPTER EIGHT

THE GREAT CAUSE

W E ALWAYS FOUND—and still find—tiresome the charge that the United States and its allies conducted the campaign in Iraq "for oil." If Iraq's oil was all we wanted, there was a very simple way to get it: lift the embargo on Iraqi oil exports. This is so obvious that we can only imagine that protesters who scream "no blood for oil" are either astonishingly stupid or cynically disingenuous.

During the 2004 presidential election campaign, the Democrats are almost certain to make the president's conduct of the war on terror an issue, and our successes thus far will somehow be rhetorically converted into defeats, with baseless charges that the president lied about the reasons for the Iraq war or that Iraq is a quagmire, and so on. In time, these fevered charges will fade, replaced, we hope, by an acknowledgment of the *fact* that the United States and its coalition parties risked much to overthrow a bloody, repressive tyranny that threatened its neighbors and killed tens of thousands of the people it ruled.

Sadly, another charge related to the Bush administration's conduct of the war on terror might have more staying power, even though it is just as baseless. Many people (among them more than a few who once had a claim to being serious) have scrutinized the men and women in the Bush administration's national security team and declared them a cabal of pro-Israel "neo-conservatives" (many of them Jews) who have hijacked U.S. national security policy in order to preserve the State of Israel and, more specifically, help the Likud Party retain its grip on power. Essentially, these critics argue, the war against radical Islamist terror is a cover. The real goal is to put the power of the United States and its allies at the disposal of Israeli Prime Minister Ariel Sharon and his Likud successors.

Israel is the most hated country in the Arab and Muslim world. The United States is the *second* most hated country in the Arab and Muslim world, the critics say, only because our government is Israel's chief supporter. Therefore, the solution to the pan-Islamist terror threat is simple: pry the neo-conservatives' hands off the tiller of U.S. foreign policy, adopt a pro-Arab policy on Palestine, and all will be well. If we abandon Israel, the pan-Islamists will no longer hate us.

This analysis is entirely untrue. The truth is, radical Islam's goals are not confined to the destruction of Israel, because radical Islam looks farther back into history and has far grander ambitions. Militant Islam has often been at war with the West—from the time of Mohammed, when Islam conquered Christian North Africa, to the end of the seventeenth century, when the Muslims were turned back from the gates of Vienna. Radical Islam is seeking to breathe new life into the history of Islamic jihad—a history of warfare against *all* nonbelievers. That is why the war on terror is a global war.

The first ambition of radical Islam is to remake the Muslim world in its own fundamentalist image. From Uzbekistan to Nigeria to Malaysia, from Kosovo to Morocco to Indonesia, the Muslim world will be returned to the "proper" militant Islamic religious, legal, political, and social order. National loyalties, they say, should mean nothing to Muslims; local and national customs and traditions should be discarded as "innovations"; and a harsh sharia law should be imposed. They see Westernized Muslim governments as corrupt, to be swept aside. Adherents to other religions, "infidels," will be put in their proper place—that is, into the status of second- and third-class citizens—or expelled or killed.

Ultimately, a pan-Islamic state would unite all Muslims and lead to the restoration of a great Islamic empire—recreating that time when the Prophet and his successors swept through the world. Once established, this empire could then turn its attention to the subjugation and conquest of the rest of the world, particularly the liberal West, as the Ottoman Turks did in the fifteenth, sixteenth, and seventeenth centuries.

Clerics educated in Saudi Arabia's ascetic Wahhabism preach this message in radical Islamic mosques from the Balkans to Berlin to Boston. Militant Islamist websites openly express contempt for "infidels" and boast of plans for a new Islamic empire. Pan-Islamic terror groups are setting up shop throughout Central Asia, often recruiting by force. Aside from attacking Indian Hindus, radical Islamists in Kashmir assault their fellow Muslims for such "crimes" as having a satellite TV dish. In Nigeria, sharia law is now the governing legal system in many states, and anti-Christian violence, often carried out by young men wearing T-shirts emblazoned with an image of Osama bin Laden, is on the upswing. In Southeast Asia, Muslim rebels have raided army camps in southern Thailand and the terrorist group Jemaah Islamiah, an Islamic militant group with links to al-Qaeda, has committed atrocities in Indonesia, including the October 2002 bombing in Bali that killed hundreds. Also, in Indonesia, the group Lashkar Jihad has sent men to regions with Christian minorities to agitate anti-Christian violence.

To say the least, Israel is not the issue here. Radical Islam is.

Our fight, however, is not against a religion. The vast majority of Muslims are obviously peaceable people. Our fight is against those who want to turn Islam into a terrorist creed preaching global violence and revolution.

What we can and must do is act against those regimes that train, shelter, and support the terrorists who are bent on killing us (Iran and Syria); put further pressure on Muslim states to curtail radical Islam within their own borders (Egypt, Pakistan); stop Muslim states from subsidizing intolerant religious belief around the world (Saudi Arabia); and demand, and bring about, an end to the WMD programs of rogue states (North Korea). We must declare a "no sanctuary for terrorists" policy and enforce it. The United States must be a faithful ally to those Muslim countries that openly oppose radical Islamist terror and that stand for tolerance and liberalization—like Morocco, Qatar, and Bahrain. Through a robust program of public diplomacy and broadcast information, the United States must promote economic, political, religious, and social freedom throughout the entire Muslim world and refute the myths about the nature of American society, politics, and culture that are rife in that world. The Five Freedoms that we've enumerated are the place to start.

In the almost two and a half years since the attacks that brought this war to our soil, the United States has brought down two bloodstained regimes of the Web of Terror. We did not fight these wars to win the next Israeli general election for Likud or even to ensure Israel's continued existence, although victory will, we hope, ensure that Israel does survive: It has that right in international law, and it is an outpost of democracy in an oppressed part of the world.

The war on terror is not a matter of law enforcement, as some politicians still seem to think. It is a war that we fight against a totalitarian ideology, like Communism, that wants to destroy Western civilization. We are, in the end, fighting this war for ourselves. And it is imperative we fight it in the right way.

In the last decade we've made tremendous progress—but it is progress that has been forced upon us. Remember that many touted the trial and conviction of the men involved in the 1993 World Trade Center bombing as a major victory in the war against terrorism. It was satisfying to be sure, but it wasn't a victory. It took the attacks of September 11, 2001, to arouse America to a better understanding of the scope of the threat. Since that day—which, like Pearl Harbor, should live in infamy—federal, state, and local governments have done much to improve domestic security, and America's intelligence and law-enforcement agencies have done great work thwarting terrorist plots. The work done to provide for the internal security of the United States is welcome, but it is not enough.

After the Axis powers declared war on the United States in December 1941, the United States did not limit its response to fortifying the Hawaiian Islands, increasing antisubmarine patrols along the Atlantic Coast, and upgrading the efforts of the FBI to crack rings of domestic Axis sympathizers and capture saboteurs. Osama bin Laden has openly and repeatedly declared war on the United States. The radical Islamists see themselves in jihad against the West, and they see the United States as the leading "Crusader" power. They see moderate Muslims who wish live in peace as traitors. Backed by state sponsors of terror like Iran, they have become a global threat just as much as the National Socialists were. Though militarily puny, their dreams and their potential danger are grandiose: inflaming a billion Muslims worldwide and creating a radical Islamist empire. To that end they will cooperate with rogue states like North Korea. They will do everything they can to acquire weapons of mass destruction.

The bottom line is that they must be stopped. End their state sponsorship, and they wither. Buttress the forces of moderate Islam, encourage freedom and tolerance in Islamic societies, grant Muslims in Iraq and Iran the opportunity to vote against tyranny and the mullahs, then the radicals do more than wither, they disappear to the fringes of Muslim society. If we are to stop the spread of radical Islam, we cannot be satisfied with the conviction of a failed terrorist bomber, dismantling a terrorist cell, or freezing the bank account of a terrorist front—however necessary all these things are. To rely purely on defensive measures cedes the initiative to the radical Islamists. Instead, we need to take the battle to them.

The counteroffensives in Afghanistan and Iraq were first steps to the endgame, they are not the endgame itself. The endgame is taking down the Web of Terror entirely so that the global terror threat dissolves. We have laid out the broad parameters of an active strategy for this war. Despite the best wishes of some, the Web of Terror cannot be talked to death, no "peace process" will work, no foreign aid will suffice unless the countries involved make a commitment—as Libya has apparently done—to forgo jihad, forgo terrorism, forgo weapons of mass destruction. Countries that will not do this willingly must be compelled to do it. Terrorism and the proliferation of weapons of mass destruction are not something we have to live with; they are something that the rogue states of the Web of Terror have to live without.

The fight is not ours alone, and it is not the West's alone. American power, American persuasion, and American might can change the regimes that support the spread of radical Islamist terror and hunt down the terrorists. But ultimately it is up to the world's Muslims to make a commitment to peace, freedom, and tolerance; to determine how they will reconcile their religion with modernity; to bring their nations more effectively into the global economy. The extinguishing of radical Islam is a project for the billion-strong Islamic world. Radical Islam is a threat to that world as much as it is a threat to the West. Promoting the Five Freedoms is our strategy for the West and moderate Islam to work together against the radicals.

Secretary Rumsfeld has characterized the war on terror as a "slog," a long, hard struggle. At times, it will seem so. It might seem so already, as the daily death toll of our soldiers in Iraq rises. But in its broad lineaments, as we have outlined in this book, the Web of Terror can be taken down—and should be taken down—swiftly. The reformation of Islam could take decades, if not centuries. Bringing democracy to the region will take years if not decades. But the primary threat, state-sponsored terror and the threat of proliferating weapons of mass destruction, can be dealt with now. To act now, in fact, is to lessen future risks. As we seek to obliterate the Web of Terror and help moderate Islam defeat its enemies (and ours), we need to remember the roots and development of our own civilization, our patriotism, our core principles. We stand armed to defend the prospect that men have the right to life, liberty, and the pursuit of happiness—and that global terrorism should not cast a pall over these inalienable rights. Sir Winston Churchill put it well when he said,

> We must recognize that we have a great inheritance in our possession, which represents the prolonged achievement of the centuries; that there is not one of our simple uncounted rights today for which better men than we are have not died on the scaffold or the battlefield. We have not only a great treasure; we have a great cause. Are we taking every measure within our power to defend that cause?

This book is our own modest effort to rally "every measure within our power to defend that cause" of peace, freedom, and prosperity.

AFTERWORD

WE HAVE PURPOSELY WRITTEN this book as a military assessment and tried to keep politics out of our analysis as much as possible. But we are frankly appalled at how all too many politicians have apparently forgotten the horror of September 11, and the proper lessons of our victories in Afghanistan and Iraq. The United States is the primary target of the Web of Terror. But we can—and must—take the Web of Terror down.

In the Democratic primaries, all the candidates except Senator Lieberman disavowed the global war on terror. They tried to deny that the Web of Terror exists. They argued that our only enemy is al-Qaeda. But where does al-Qaeda live? In how many nations are its terror cells embedded? From where does al-Qaeda draw its support?

We have provided the answers in this book.

Unfortunately, not everyone wants to face the answers. For example, France, Russia, Germany, and the United Nations were all complicit in trying to keep Saddam Hussein in power. For the Europeans, Saddam was a trading partner. For the United Nations, he was a cash cow. We now have records documenting that 270 companies, organizations, and individuals in fifty countries benefited from the UN-operated Oil-for-Food program in Iraq; for them, the continuation of sanctions and Saddam Hussein in power meant the continuation of a substantial flow of money. Anyone who suggests that we should have waited for United Nations approval to remove Saddam Hussein is effectively saying that the world would be a better place with Saddam Hussein still in power in Iraq.

The benefits of removing Saddam Hussein are now flowing in. Libya has renounced weapons of mass destruction and expressed its desire for reconciliation with the West, and is even discussing possible peace talks with Israel. Pakistan has started to confess, investigate, and stop its nuclear weapons proliferation to Iran, Libya, and North Korea, and has announced peace talks with India. Iran's reformist-minded majority is growing ever more bold and defiant against the tyrannical mullahs. Syria has made tentative steps toward cooperation with the West. The list of benefits that have come from toppling Saddam Hussein continues to grow. But let's not be complacent, as Iran's rush to develop a nuclear weapons capability before our presidential elections is a major threat to the U.S. and to stability in the region.

There is still tough fighting ahead in Iraq and Afghanistan. But the jihadists know they are losing. In February 2004, a memo came to light that appears to be written by Abu Mus'ab al-Zarqawi, a terrorist affiliated with al-Qaeda and now in Iraq, to al-Qaeda's high command. In that memo, he writes, "We can pack up and leave and look for another land, just like it has happened in so many lands of jihad. Our enemy is growing stronger day after day, and its intelligence information increases. By God, this is suffocation!" The main battle is in Iraq, and al-Qaeda is losing it.

The Web of Terror will want to influence America's presidential elections because the Web of Terror will not survive four more years of George W. Bush. When critics of the war in Iraq say that Iraq will become "another Vietnam," we reply that will happen only if antiwar politicians achieve the power to make it so and appease the Web of Terror.

We have written this book to inform America of the dangers and opportunities ahead. Let us be united when it comes to guaranteeing our nation's security and eliminating the Web of Terror. Preserving American lives should not be a partisan issue.

REPORTING FROM THE SCENE

WE HAD THE OPPORTUNITY to meet with important leaders of the Middle East, including Lt. General Shaul Mofaz, Israel's minister of defense, and his royal highness, Reza Pahlavi, son of the former shah of Iran.

Our visit to Israel in July 2003, organized by the AIFL (America-Israel Friendship League), has been critical to our understanding of why the "roadmap to peace" will not succeed unless Iran, Syria, and Saudi Arabia stop funding terror. As long as Hamas, Hezbollah, and other major terrorist groups are funded and led from this Web of Terror, peace is impossible—something one sees readily on the ground in the Middle East.

We also went on the scene to Iraq in September 2003, at the invitation of Secretary of Defense Donald Rumsfeld and saw for ourselves the extraordinary progress our troops have made not only to free the country but to rebuild it.

October 9, 2002: **Note: For security reasons, the face of the man in the center is obscured.** As the possibility of liberating Iraq was looming, Lt. General Shaul Mofaz (left), the then-retired chief of staff of the Israeli defense forces, met in Washington, D.C., with Lt. General Tom McInerney to discuss war plans for potential operations in Iraq. Here General Mofaz expressed his concerns about chemical or biological attacks on Israel and the possibility that Israel would be drawn into the war by such attacks. Fortunately, Lt. General McInerney's prediction of a quick victory (less than thirty days), followed by no major urban warfare in Baghdad and no WMD attacks on Israel, came true. They also discussed the urgency of dealing with the potential of a nuclear-armed Iran and the danger this presented not only to Israel, but to the world. Within weeks of this meeting, General Mofaz became Israel's minister of defense.

On January 4, 2004, Minister of Defense Mofaz publicly declared that Iran's nuclear capabilities presented the gravest ever danger to Israel's survival. His remarks were echoed by General Meir Dagan, chief of the Mossad (Israeli intelligence service), in an unprecedented meeting with the Knesset foreign affairs and defense committee.

Note: For security reasons, the face of the man on the right is obscured. Reza Pahlavi (center), the former crown prince of Iran, and Lt. Gen. McInerney met to discuss the growing nuclear threat that Iran is presenting to stability in the region. His wise advice is used throughout this book. He has our best wishes that he help lead a free and democratic Iran.

Maj. Gen. Paul Vallely; Col. Jack Jacobs, MSNBC News military analyst; and Lt. Gen. Tom McInerney meet during their July 7–13, 2003,
visit to Israel.

Ra'anan Gissin, spokesman for Prime Minister Sharon, briefs Maj. General Vallely, Lt. Gen. McInerney, and Col. Jacobs on the current status of the
"roadmap to peace."

(Seated L to R), Lt. General McInerney, Maj. General Vallely, and Col. Jacobs, are briefed by Nezah Mashiah, head of the Seam Line Project (Israel's security wall) and other Israeli Defense Force personnel.

(L to R) Nezah Mashiah, Col. Jacobs, Lt. General McInerney, an Israel Defense Force (IDF) Lt. Col., and Maj. General Vallely view the security wall at a West Bank checkpoint.

Nezah Mashiah and Maj. General
Vallely discuss the construction of
Israel's security fence. In the center
is Bill Behrer, AIFL director of communications, who hosted the visit of
the military analysts.

This picture shows a State Department official (who was responsible
for documenting the mass graves in
Iraq) standing in front of the graves
of 400,000 dead near Hila. There
have been more than 30,000 such
mass graves discovered to date.

Mass gravesite near Hila, Iraq,
that contained 3,000 Shi'ite men,
women, and children. The horrific
evidence of the mass graves alone
justified Operation Iraqi Freedom.

Lt. General McInerney in front of the coalition provisional authority
headquarters in the Green Zone prior to going downtown to the FOX News
Channel studios in Baghdad. Note that the right wing of the palace has no
roof, yet the rest of the building is fully operational. Smart bombs work!
September 22, 2003.

(L to R) Maj. General Viggers, British Army deputy commander; Lt. General
Sanchez, US Army commander CJTF7; and Col. Hicks, US Army J-3 CICS; brief
Lt. General McInerney and other military analysts at coalition provisional
authority headquarters September 2003.

Two unidentified female guides were thrilled to show our group the magnificently restored ancient city of Babylon during our September 20–25, 2003,
visit to Iraq, as part of the first group the secretary of defense sponsored to
visit Iraq.

Ishtar Gate (replica) in Babylon, Iraq. The original is in the Pergamon Museum in Berlin. Saddam Hussein restored this magnificent gate as part of his efforts to restore the monuments and artifacts of ancient Babylon. One hour south of Baghdad near the town of Hila, it will make a wonderful tourist attraction in the coming years.

Lt. General McInerney and Maj. General Vallely stand in front of a map of ancient
Babylon after a tour of the site on September 23, 2003.

(L to R) Maj. General Vallely; Maj. General Tyszkiewicz, Polish commander of the multinational division (MND), and Lt. General McInerney pose during our visit to the MND in September 2003. The MND was replacing the 1st Marine Division, which was rotating back to the U.S.

Maj. General Ray Odierno standing on the extreme left in front of his 4th
Infantry Division headquarters in Tikrit, Iraq. This palace complex, the largest
in Iraq, includes more than 170 buildings. The UN's Oil-for-Food Program
helped support such extravangances.

Old Glory flies in a C-130 transport aircraft flown by the Air National Guard. In the field, our National Guard and Reserve forces are indistinguishable from the regulars and are playing a vital role in our success in Iraq.

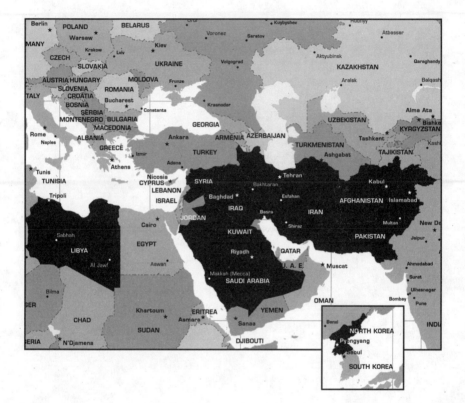

ACKNOWLEDGMENTS

WE BOTH FEEL TRULY BLESSED TO have had the opportunity to write a book that we believe is so important to the future of America. Obviously we owe a great debt of gratitude to many people and many organizations that each played a part in our role as military analysts.

We owe a thank-you to the FOX News Channel team and contributors, Roger Ailes, Brit Hume, Tony Snow, Bill O'Reilly, Neil Cavuto, Sean Hannity, Alan Colmes, Greta Van Sustren, John Gibson, Linda Vester, Rita Cosby, Geraldo Rivera, Steve Doocy, E. D. Hill, Brian Kilmeade, David Asman, Jon Scott, Julian Phillips, Juliet Huddy, Lauren Green, Bob Sellers, Eric Shawn, Laurie Dhue, Molly Henneberg, Kelly Wright, Jim Angle, Jerry Burke, Brian Wilson, Bret Baier, Ken "The Brain Room" Dudonis, Marty Ryan, Matt Singerman, Kevin Magee, John Moody, Shepard Smith, Mike Jerrick, Gregg Jarrett, Thom Bird, Bill Shine, Griff Jenkins, Jane Skinner, Dianne Brandi, Kiran Chetry, Patti Ann Browne, Bridget Quinn, Page Hopkins, Dari Alexander, Judge Andrew Napolitana, Rich O'Brien and the FOX graphics department, Amy Burkholder, the FOX booking staff, producers, directors, makeup departments, and the remainder of the FOX team, whose behind-the-scenes efforts come together to make each show a success.

We would like to particularly give our gratitude to talk-show hosts John Batchelor and Paul Alexander of WABC of New York; Alan Nathan, Jane Silk, Greg Corombus, and Blanquita Cullum of RadioAmerica; John Stokes of K600, Kalispell, Montana; Erich "Mancow" Muller of Q101 of Chicago; and Monica Crowley of WABC NY.

Also thanks to Charles Krauthammer, Bill Kristol, Fred Barnes, Mort Kondracke, Juan Williams, and Jim Woolsey.

A special thank-you goes to Oliver North for writing the introduction and for the opportunity to guest on his radio show many times. In particular we would like to thank him for his dedication to this country and for going back into the combat zone at this stage of his life, exposing himself to great risk during Operation Iraqi Freedom. His insights and battlefield reports as an embedded reporter were invaluable to our analysis.

We would also like to thank who we call our "first embedded reporter in Afghanistan," Steven Harrigan. And thanks to Greg Kelly and Rick Leventhal, the first embedded reporters in Iraq. Also to Jennifer Griffin in Jerusalem; Steve Centanni, James Rosen at the White House, Kelly Wright, Major Garrett, Wendell Goler, Jim Angle, Bill Tobin, Bob Armfield, Mark "Bubba" White, Bill Gertz, Rowan Scarborough, Frank Gaffney, and Jed Babbin.

A special acknowledgment to Scott Belliveau, our writer, who spent countless weeks and months working with us on this prodigious task. It could not have been done without him and we are deeply grateful.

And thanks to Marji Ross, president of Regnery Publishing, for giving us this opportunity, and to our editors, Harry Crocker and Miriam Moore, who worked so closely with us as we went to final production.

And finally, we would like to thank our other fellow military analysts, Captain (USN Ret) Chuck Nash, Lt. Col. Bill Cowan, Col. David Hunt, Maj. Bob Bevelacqua, Maj. General Burt Moore, Maj. General Bob Scales, Lt. Col. Bob McGinnis, Lt. Col. Tim Eads, Command Sgt. Major Steve Greer, Don Edwards, Dennis Ross of Mansoor Ijaz Radio,

Mark Ginsberg, Entifadh Qanbar, Tim Trevane, General Najeb al Salhi, Avi Ben-Abraham, and Waria al Salhi.

FOR FURTHER READING

See No Evil: The True Story of a Ground Soldier in the CIA's Counterterrorism Wars, by Robert Baer (Crown Publishers, 2002)

Sleeping with the Devil: How Washington Sold Our Soul for Saudi Crude, by Robert Baer (Crown Publishers, 2003)

Why We Fight: Moral Clarity and the War on Terrorism, by William J. Bennett (Regnery Publishing, 2003)

Brighter Than the Baghdad Sun: Saddam Hussein's Nuclear Threat to the United States, by Shyam Bhatia and Daniel McGrory (Regnery Publishing, 2000)

The Lessons of Terror: A History of Warfare Against Civilians, by Caleb Carr (Random House, 2003)

Terrorism, Afghanistan, and America's New Way of War, by Norman Friedman (Naval Institute Press, 2003)

A Peace to End All Peace: Creating the Modern Middle East, 1914–1922, by David Fromkin (Henry Holt, 1989)

Breakdown: How America's Intelligence Failures Led to September 11, by Bill Gertz (Regnery Publishing, 2002)

Hatred's Kingdom: How Saudi Arabia Supports the New Global Terrorism, by Dore Gold (Regnery Publishing, 2003)

Carnage and Culture: Landmark Battles in the Rise to Western Power, by Victor Davis Hanson (Anchor, 2002)

An Autumn of War: What America Learned from September 11 and the War on Terrorism, by Victor Davis Hanson (Anchor, 2002)

The War against the Terror Masters: Why It Happened, Where We Are Now, How We'll Win, by Michael A. Ledeen (St. Martin's Press, 2002)

Legacy: Paying the Price for the Clinton Years, by Rich Lowry (Regnery Publishing, 2003)

Transformation Under Fire: Revolutionizing How America Fights, by Douglas Macgregor (Praeger Publishers, 2003)

Losing Bin Laden: How Bill Clinton's Failures Unleashed Global Terror, by Richard Miniter (Regnery Publishing, 2003)

War Stories: Operation Iraqi Freedom, by Oliver North (Regnery Publishing, 2003)

The Crusaders, by Regine Pernoud (Ignatius Press, 2003)

Beyond Baghdad: Postmodern War and Peace, by Ralph Peters (Stackpole, 2003)

Taliban: Militant Islam, Oil, and Fundamentalism in Central Asia, by Ahmed Rashid (Yale University Press, 2000)

Jihad: The Rise of Militant Islam in Central Asia, by Ahmed Rashid (Yale University Press, 2002)

What Were the Crusades?, by Jonathan Riley-Smith (Ignatius Press, 2003)

Yasir Arafat: A Political Biography, by Barry Rubin and Judith Colp Rubin (Oxford University Press, 2003)

Fighting Back: The War on Terrorism from Inside the Bush White House, by Bill Sammon (Regnery Publishing, 2002)

The March Up: Taking Baghdad with the 1st Marine Division, by Ray L. Smith and Bing West (Bantam, 2003)

The Mystery of Capital: Why Capitalism Triumphs in the West and Fails Everywhere Else, by Hernando de Soto (Basic Books, 2000)

Onward Muslim Soldiers: How Jihad Still Threatens America and the West, by Robert Spencer (Regnery Publishing, 2003)

Boots on the Ground: A Month with the 82nd Airborne in the Battle for Iraq, by Karl Zinsmeister (Truman Talley Books, 2003)

INDEX